MITCHELL/GIURGOLA ARCHITECTS

MITCHELL/GIURGOLA ARCHITECTS

Ehrman B. Mitchell
Romaldo Giurgola

FOREWORD BY KENNETH FRAMPTON

RIZZOLI
NEW YORK

Published in the United States of America in 1983 by
RIZZOLI INTERNATIONAL PUBLICATIONS, INC.
712 Fifth Avenue, New York, New York, 10019

Library of Congress Cataloging in Publication Data
Main entry under title:

Mitchell /Giurgola Architects.

  "Bibliography of Romaldo Giurgola writings": p.
  Bibliography: p.
  Includes index.
  1. Mitchell/Giurgola Architects. 2. Architecture,
Modern—20th century—United States. I. Mitchell,
Ehrman B. II. Giurgola, Romaldo. III. Title.
NA737.M57M58 1983   720'.92'2   83-42909
ISBN 0-8478-0495-X (pbk.)

Typeset in the United States of America
Printed by Mandarin Offset International, Ltd., Hong Kong

ACKNOWLEDGMENTS

The production of this book has been a project of many years' duration. Because the layout of each page was designed and completed within our architectural office, the book has become a labor of love touching all of us, whether partners or young architects or administrative staff. To acknowledge the work of particular members of our office does not deny the contributions of all to the book's completion. But without the efforts of a team composed of Romaldo Giurgola, Ehrman Mitchell, Pamille Berg, Amy Anderson, Carol Loewenson, Scott Phillips, Nancy Brandenburg, Dennis Berg, Karen Lennox, Sharon Moore and Charlotte Present, the book would never have come to be. Without Rollin La France's photographs of many of our buildings during the past twenty years, the book would be a far less complete documentation of our work. A special recognition and thanks is given to Pamille Berg for her long-standing and selfless involvement with this publication.

This volume is dedicated to all of the members of our office, past and present, to whom this work belongs, both in spirit and in fact.

FOREWORD

Kenneth Frampton

It may not be amiss for the architect to take advantage *sometimes* of that to which I am sure the painter ought always to have his eyes open, I mean the use of accidents; to follow where they lead and to improve them, rather than always trust to a regular plan.

Sir Joshua Reynolds
Thirteenth discourse at the Royal Academy
11 December 1786

Ehrman Mitchell and Romaldo Giurgola have been long regarded as representatives of the Philadelphia School, although clearly they, like the other pupils and colleagues of Louis Kahn, have found the late modern master difficult to follow. Thus, despite his homage to Kahn—the book *Louis Kahn* of 1975, written with Jaimini Mehta—Giurgola's own work has tended to side-step the direct influence of the Philadelphia master. As a result, apart from a number of diminutively scaled and exquisite urban works—the Philadelphia Life Insurance Company addition (1962), the Philadelphia subway concourse entrance (1971), and the Liberty Bell Pavilion (1975)—Giurgola seems to have deliberately distanced himself from Kahn's preoccupation with the monumentality of structural form and construction. Giurgola's empathy for the social democratic policies of postwar Europe no doubt helped to remove him from Kahn's commitment to the cultural aims of the American New Monumentality.[1] Nonetheless there appears at the outset of his career a brilliant work which comes remarkably close to Kahn's passion for structural expressiveness. This is Giurgola's second prize entry for the Boston City Hall Competition of 1962; a design whose compositional authority and sense of structural hierarchy was certainly superior to that of the winning scheme. Moreover unlike Kallman, McKinnell and Knowles's spectacular but conventionally Brutalist city hall, Giurgola's project (designed in collaboration with David Crane and Tim Vreeland) evoked the robust forms of the Boston Back Bay brick tradition while amplifying, in a manner appropriate to the megalopolitan scale of the late twentieth century, something of the generosity and civic grandeur which was once associated with H.H. Richardson's Trinity Church of 1876. And while Giurgola's City Hall may at first appear to be as Brutalist as the premiated design, its style remained refreshingly aloof from the *béton brut* manner to which it was indebted; that is to say, Giurgola transformed the syntax which he drew, in part, from Le Corbusier's monastery at La Tourette completed in 1960. The most dramatic shift in this regard is the way in which he changed Le Corbusier's *brise soleil* more into a structural wall or diaphragm spanning between supporting access towers.

Mitchell/Giurgola have distanced their work from Kahn in a variety of ways. In the first instance they seem to have been attracted to the more superficial aspects of the New Monumentality, as this appeared in the more structurally ostentatious works of Eero Saarinen. This tendency announced itself briefly in their Wright Brothers Memorial Visitors Center, built in Kill Devil Hills, North Carolina in 1960. Soon after, however, they shifted their affinities to the more organic side of European Brutalism; to that complex sensibility, typified by Aalto's House of Culture, built in Helsinki in 1958 and by Stirling and Gowan's Leicester Engineering Laboratory completed in 1963. These referential poles crop up repeatedly throughout the early years of the practice. Thus there is clearly something of Stirling's Queens College Oxford (1966) in the MDRT Foundation Hall built at Bryn Mawr, Pennsylvania, in 1972 and the same influence is surely to be found in the canted, curtain-wall of Giurgola's ill-fated proposal for the AIA Headquarters of 1971. By the same token, Aalto's Baker House of 1948, is clearly latent in the spread-eagled layout of the Mission Park Students dormitory built at Williamstown in 1972, although its staggered cells and interior detailing owe much to Stirling's St.Andrews University complex of 1964. Aalto's influence is again detectable in the interiors of Giurgola's lecture halls and libraries as one may judge from, say, the Lang Music Building, Swarthmore (1973) or the Tredyffrin Public Library, built at Strafford, Pennsylvania in 1976.

Aside from this organicism more local influences are evident in Mitchell/Giurgola's work; on the one hand, Colin Rowe's collagist approach to urban form, as elaborated in Cornell University, on the other, an affinity for *cardboard architecture,* that is to say, for that approach to architecture facilitated by the wooden balloon frame and manipulated to diverse ends by Robert Venturi, Charles Moore and the Five Architects. Although Giurgola has rarely built in timber he has nonetheless exploited the scenographic aspects of this approach in the thin screen facades that often adorn his larger buildings as in, say, the prefabricated tile-faced, concrete panelling which covers the perimeter duct manifolds of the Sherman Fairchild Life Sciences Building, erected on the Columbia University campus in 1977. And yet for all of the potential freedom afforded by such facades Mitchell/Giurgola still resorted to Kahnian principles for the underlying order of their plans; that is to say, they turned to the superimposition of disjunctive geometries wherein a rotated square or triangle may be used to generate dynamic spaces in an orthogonal grid or where semicircular or circular voids would be cut into square or triangular masses in order to liberate the interstitial space. Giurgola was able to reconcile this Kahnian geometry with the *collagisme* of his screen facades through the cultivation of a picturesque sensibility and this synthetic strategy is fully evolved by the time of the Columbus East High School of 1973.

Throughout the seventies the structuring of compositions about this idea of an internal "narrative landscape" colors the work of the office irrespective of the context. Such an attitude finds confirmation in Giurgola's writing: "I have come to think of architecture as an episode, as a fragment of an itinerary. A building is no more than a fragment of the fabric of our environment, a fragment seeking the measure of its relationship with other elements: trees, water, meadows, sky, other buildings, or other open spaces of the city."[2] This notion of a building being made up of a series of picturesque incidents—a concept related to the modernist principles of disjunctive composition and *bricollage*—also imparts a musical connotation Giurgola's work. This he acknowledges when he refers to fragments which ". . . [must be] composed in such a way that they allow a continuity between episodes . . . one who walks through them should feel, as in a poem or in music, as if one is in the midst of an endless environment."[3] Removed from the conventional idea of architecture as "frozen music" this approach seems to have been at variance with the classical precepts which were otherwise present in Giurgola's work. Hence in his comment that: "Today we perceive nature in its constant mutations; the Greeks could freeze the acanthus leaves in their capitals. The spaces of the past were related to an immutable condition. We perceive our spaces as related to the possible; firm in their evocation, and yet as elements of an itinerary which links far distant situations."[4]

This picturesque sensibility has served Giurgola well in the planning of university campuses since it has enabled him to introduce geometric and topographic inflections at will. The concept of a fragmented itinerary has allowed him to insert an ascending stairway here or a diagonal promenade there and to use such devices as a way of advancing the spatial narrative of highly attenuated complexes. This practice bestows an ontological depth on his work; a kind of tactile layering into the site which seems at odds with the sudden introduction of large scenographic planes, used, as in the Columbus East High School, to terminate the linear thrust of extended compositions.

Mitchell/Giurgola's site planning is at its most poetic and evocative where the landscape itself is particularly strong and where it is related in a direct way to primal cosmic elements. Thus as Giurgola has recently written of the Swedish landscape: "In Sweden the sea appears as a hint of vastness, framed by the dark masses of spruces, merging gradually with the growth of the green foliage. Places are naturally formed by wooded hills surrounding the flat meadow, open at one end toward the sea, where the encounter with the elements is subtle but full of wonder, full of expectations; the shelter never betraying the place."[5]

For all this hypersensitivity to the *genius loci* it is sometimes difficult to discern what has motivated the overall structure in some of Mitchell/Giurgola's larger layouts, particularly where the topography, the existing access and the planting fail to account for the overall composition. On occasion their campus planning borders on formal indifference. This lack of focus becomes most disturbing when the buildings themselves assume different morphologies, as in the case of the American College Campus at Bryn Mawr, Pennsylvania, under development from 1966 to 1981.

For the critic, on the other hand, Giurgola's work at Bryn Mawr permits a reading of his stylistic evolution over a decade revealing a shift from the Brutalist syntax of the Foundation Hall (1972) to the more sophisticated, Expressionist scheme adopted in the Graduate Center (1981) whose dynamic composition is more intimately related with the ground. This stylistic shift is not only evident across the decade but is also perceivable within the design itself, for clearly the finished building differs significantly from the schematic Giurgola perspective which established the initial massing. As Giurgola modestly admits it is not always possible to determine whether a particular realization comes into being as a result of individual development or whether it emerges out of the procedures of teamwork. In any event, there is no doubt that the Graduate Center at Bryn Mawr is one of the finest works which Mitchell/Giurgola have produced to date.

Since the Foundation Hall (1972) is faced in tile and the Graduate Center (1981) is clad in brick the formal differences which obtain between them merit analysis, for where the detailing of the former is abstract and minimalist— that is to say, where the fenestration is set proud of the masonry throughout, so as to appear as though it were floating and weightless—the latter contains the glazing within the body of the masonry, the architect often choosing to withdraw the glass from the face. This displacement in the glazing plane has consequences for the respective skins of the two buildings for where the Graduate Center expresses its floor levels through the use of continuous horizontal string courses in colored tilework (the latter is also used to face the perimeter piers), the tilework of the Foundation Hall is treated as an indifferentiated skin. It is just such distinctions, at the level of detail, which, by way of contrast, gives greater tectonic animation to the sweep and thrust of the dynamic forms from which the Graduate Center is composed; the quadrant housing, the dining facilities and the semicircular, glass-brick enclosures to the stair-towers which terminate the residential slab. Such is the formal authority of the complementary detailing—for example, the tubular steel parapet railing to the quadrant or the rotational sweep of the tubular steelwork of the terrace stairway and pergola—that one is reminded of Mendelsohn and of the way this exemplary architect was able to enrich and strengthen his work through horizontal emphasis. Faced with a work of such extraordinary richness and formal energy one reflects on the demagogic absurdity of today's reaction against all modern form; of the irresponsibility of those who carp at the reductive nature of modern architecture without fully evaluating the movement in terms of its more elaborate and poetic achievements.

Like Aalto before them, Mitchell/Giurgola have often been at their best in libraries and this building type has invariably enabled them to achieve works of exceptional quality. The dynamic radial volume of the Tredyffrin Public Library is a case in point, although the colossal Davis Research Library, recently completed at Chapel Hill, North Carolina, is even more integrated in terms of tectonic order, even if its internal volume is largely indifferentiated. One of the most sensitive pieces of urban infill in Giurgola's career also happens to be a library; the ingenuously sited, domestically-scaled and delicately proportioned South End Library built in Boston in 1970. The single most felicitous aspect of this work is surely the perimeter pergola which is used not only to establish the public character of the forecourt but also to represent the institutional status of the building. At the other end of the scale the Davis Research Library is a self-contained megastructure; one which seems to assume the form of an antique aqueduct as it spans across the modestly dimensioned blocks of the Chapel Hill campus. This is surely the most Kahnian work yet achieved by the Mitchell/Giurgola practice, above all for the articulation of its "carrel towers" which line up like vast pylons, along the southern flank of the bookstack-slab.

A great deal of the practice of Mitchell/Giurgola has been devoted to the working environment and as one would expect in an age dominated by bureaucracy, most of their efforts in this regard have been expended on the design of office buildings. Needless to say, this type is by now so determined by the economy as to leave little room for innovation at the level of spatial organization. As with other architects the imperatives of the type have had the effect of transforming the style of the office since the combined pressures of speculation and technological economy have invariably favored the adoption of modular, constructional techniques. Thus the high-tech, neoprene-gasketted curtain wall which was only an option in the mid-sixties has since become a normative technique and this is reflected in the changing attitude of the Giurgola practice towards the design of the high-rise office building. This would account for the move away from the more figurative and sculptural approach displayed in the United Way Headquarters, Philadelphia of 1971 towards the hermetic skin of the Two INA Plaza development of 1975. Aside from the provision of an articulated cornice element and the symmetrical treatment of the mid-point service floor INA Plaza is largely indistinguishable in its syntax from the high-tech revetment perfected by the school of Saarinen in the late sixties. Indeed the narrow horizontal glazing of Two INA Plaza is almost the exact inverse of the profiling and fenestration adopted by Cesar Pelli for his Oakland City Center of 1971.

In that it is a categoric reinterpretation of the standard type, the Ten Stamford Forum development, built at Stamford, Connecticut in 1979, is in many ways the most progressive office building realized by the firm to date. It is hard to imagine something more needed by the current exigencies of provincial city development than a building which integrates the parking garage with the high-rise element and this synthesis is formally unified at Stamford by the provision of a monumental, twelve storey, chamfered recession in the main facade. This symmetrical setback, combined with a two-storey circular opening let into one wing of the parking podium transforms the entire complex into a giant piece of "minimalist" sculpture and this effect depends on the supression of the structure. One notes that, as in the Saarinen School, Mitchell/Giurgola office buildings rarely expose the frame as a tectonic element, in contradistinction to Kahn's suspended office tower projected for Kansas City in 1966.

The practice's most significant contribution to the work-place has surely been made in the domain of industry, above all in the Volvo Assembly Plant built at Chesapeake, Virginia in 1976 and in the Lukens Steel Company administration building realized in Coatesville, Pennsylvania in 1979. Curiously enough, from an expressive standpoint, the latter is the more Scandinavian of the two, inasmuch as its *parti* is indebted equally to Aalto and Asplund—to Aalto for the compositional device of ordering irregular masses against a straight line (as in Aalto's Leverkusen Cultural Center project of 1962) and to Asplund for the deployment of a series of free-standing orthogonal pavilions, running in front of a supressed mass, as in the funerary chapel entrances to the Woodland Cemetery Crematorium, Stockholm, of 1940. Where Volvo was a somewhat predictable exercise in high-tech, modular, factory construction, the Lukens complex is a more symbolic work, composed of two primary forms; the first, a segmental, *burolandshaft* block enclosing an inner forecourt, the second (within the forecourt itself), an alternating sequence of cubic pavilions, separated by patios and united by a pierced, single-storey, frontal screen. This dynamic bipartite arrangement surely makes Lukens one of the most elegant and efficiently planned administration buildings erected in recent years, above all perhaps for the egalitarian way in which the office landscape is integrated with the directoral suite and its ancilliaries.

Mitchell/Giurgola have had ample opportunity to demonstrate their capacity as urban designers, first in two successive studies for a hotel/retail complex at Westlake Park, Seattle (1977 and 1980) and then in an office-cum-retail complex built for Harrisburg, Pennsylvania in 1979. As far as downtown development is concerned the Harrisburg complex, known as Strawberry Square, is surely the largest and most successful contextual piece carried out by the office, largely because unlike the Wainwright State Office complex built in St. Louis of 1980, it successfully relates to the quite varied architectural scales obtaining in the vicinity and to diverse focii of urban quality and interest; in this instance the State Capitol and adjoining park, the pedestrianized Strawberry Street and a cross axis bisecting the development known as Dewberry Street.

On the other hand, Westlake Park was clearly the more ambitious of the two schemes, both urbanistically and architecturally, for it sought to introduce a new form of "social condenser" into the heart of a downtown district. This is particularly true of the first version which in certain respects seems to have harked back to the spatio-mechanical concepts of the Russian constructivist avant-garde. From a compositional point of view, Westlake would have been both pure and impure; pure in its focus on the central symmetrical plaza, impure in the way this centroid would have been inflected towards the various countervailing urban incidents impinging on the site. This dynamic constructivist aspect, atypical in Giurgola's work, was eliminated from the second version of Westlake, where the plaza was handled in a more classical manner.

The last four years have seen a major shift in the house-style, so much so that the firm now seems to be on the verge of abandoning the hybrid, post-Kahnian, collagist approach which informed its production over the past fifteen years. This, as yet, unconsolidated change has assumed two forms, on the one hand it has led, at least in Giurgola's Italian work, to the assumption of a typological approach, inasmuch as the Italian buildings (in particular the Technical High School at Maniago and the Student Housing at San Pietro al Natisone, both completed in 1981) have been designed as traditional courtyard structures, with low-pitched, tiled roofs and short projecting wings, separated by patios. On the other hand, as in some of their more recent university work, Mitchell/Giurgola's compositions have tended to be organized symmetrically about axial emblematic forms, based on motifs drawn from the Art Deco period. This last is evident in the gable ends of the Swarthmore Physical Activities Building of 1979. A similar centralized stepping pattern also determines the revetment adopted in the C.W. Post Center, theater renovation, completed at Long Island University, Greenvale, New York, in 1981.

While these potentially antithetical approaches (the typological *parti* and the emblematic facade) have been successfully synthesized by other architects (see for example the recent work of Mario Botta) they seem to present themselves here as divergent positions from which to develop the expressive range of the office. At first glance these formal approaches seem to sit awkwardly with the picturesque sensibility, although Mitchell/Giurgola have made attempts recently to synthesize all three aspects, the picturesque, the typological and the decorative. This is perhaps best achieved in their designs for the Volvo corporate headquarters scheduled for completion in 1984 on a site outside Gothenburg, Sweden.

This integration of the picturesque with plan types and elevational systems which make classical references, reaches its apotheosis in Giurgola's monumental, "anti-monument"; his prize-winning design for the new Australian Parliament House, now under construction. With this work his career comes full circle and the fact that his first design of consequence was a governmental building now seems to have been portentous. It is, of course a far cry from a city hall to a parliament house and yet despite obvious differences in size and appointment, certain similarities between these works are revealing. What Boston and Canberra have most in common is the fact that both buildings are foursquare compositions, the one predicated on an incomplete square, the other spread-eagled across an orthogonal *templum*. The Australian work is inscribed in a vast traffic circle, whose axes are geomantically related to the four cardinal points. Aside from this origin in generative geometry, the divergent nature of these works is in the last analysis of greater consequence, for where Boston is asymmetrically inflected, Canberra is strictly symmetrical and where the one is structurally expressive, the other consummates the typological, classic manner of the mature Giurgola; that is to say, it is carried out in a reduced trabeated manner, with strong affinities for the Italian Tendenza. And yet where the City Hall displayed an uninhibited monumentality, the Parliament House remains an ambivalent monument. This last difference stems from the primary expressive role which the City Hall project assigned to structure whereas the Parliament House confines all significant expression to the articulation of its plastic form. This is most noticeable in the principal chamber of the Parliament itself where the prime structural supports are either half-screened or rendered in an ambivalent way. Moreover where the City Hall was designated, like the Palazzo della Signoria in Florence, to be embedded within a dense urban fabric, the Parliament House is a topographic citadel, rooted in the semi-suburban megalopolis which Walter Burley Griffin's Canberra has become.

The Parliament House's science-fiction appearance from the air, is not without significance and certain historic precedents immediately come to mind; Palmanova, Versailles and, perhaps, more recently, the cylindrical hub of Charles de Gaulle airport. None of these associations can be regarded as fortuitous since all three are or rather were strategical centers of power and communication. Aside from these precedents, Giurgola's Parliament House will surely assume its place in that line of twentieth century parliament buildings which are continental rather than urban in their scope of reference.

The elaborate earthworks and landscape which surround the Parliament House in Canberra are regarded by the architect as symbolically reaffirming the romantic mainspring of the Enlightenment; namely, that democratic legitimacy and power have a natural, almost cosmic origin. The rhetoric of Giurgola's quadripartite plan implies that a parliament comprised of an upper and lower house is naturally legitimised, with the House of Representatives facing east, the Senate facing west and the Executive facing south. The ceremonial entry forecourt to the north receives Griffin's original land axis of 1913—a direct evocation of nature as a mythic force—running out across ornamental water via a grand tree-lined avenue towards the Old Parliament Building, the War Memorial and the distant Mount Ainslie. The intent of reinforcing this axis, through aligning the center of Parliament with a series of other minor peaks extending in a straight line from Mount Ainslie to Mount Bimberi is commented on in Giurgola's gloss to a schematic sketch which reads: "the primary task in this design has been the search for a relationship of balance and reciprocity between the imposition of government and the natural state from which government evolves."

In contrast to this deference to the symbolic connotations of Griffin's land axis the symmetrical composition adopted in each quadrant (cf. Lukens *parti*) respectfully unifies the Representatives, the Senators and the Executive body about central axes focused on differently pitched tiled roofs which are supposed to express in arbitrary form the character of these "checks and balances." The potential monumentality of these plastic inflections, including the bow-fronted screen to the northern forecourt, is held in check by the organic trajectory of the concrete retaining walls which run behind each of the opposing quadrants. These elliptical earthworks rising towards the center and backed up by berms of diminishing width are finally the only unequivocally monumental feature in the entire composition. It is no accident that as these walls attain their maximum height they thicken out to provide support to the superstructure of the flag pole reminiscent of Venturi's use of a giant flag in his Thousand Oaks project. This somewhat contentious imperial flag

will be constantly visible as a symbol through the glazed roof of the members' meeting hall below. Clearly Griffin's proposal for crowning the hill with a Humanist dome has been deliberately abandoned here in favor of a "dematerialized" superstructure.

The strength of Giurgola's design can only be finally appreciated on the site itself where the building assumes the status of an artificial acropolis and where the colossal elliptical concrete berms draw the all but invisible geometry of Griffin's City Beautiful plan into three-dimensional relief. This elevated view of the city is best obtained from the raised public concourse which, while interpenetrating the multistory meeting chambers on every side, also provides for distant vistas over the low foothills which surround Canberra. This felicitous conjunction evokes a triple reading of both the institution and its site. In the first place the visiting public may, symbolically at least, watch over the workings of its parliament, in the second they may perceive the very concourse on which they stand as the keystone of Griffin's capital city, while in the third place, the distant view of the foothills gives to this privileged plateau the sense that it is indeed a continental center and that out there beyond the enclosing and still slightly ominous gum tree bush there lies the vast expanse of the continent to which the proceedings of this hub must ultimately refer.

If, as Robert Stern asserts, "Giurgola's most satisfying works are often his most modest," then how should one evaluate a practice that has been so consistently dedicated to the achievement of large public buildings? One might go so far as to claim that Mitchell/Giurgola alone among the large production offices of the American scene have suceeded in creating a large body of *public* work which is sensitive, appropriate, economic and beautifully built. Unlike those firms which have earned their reputation on the basis of giant and often brilliant pieces of minimalist sculpture—realized in the main for prestige corporations and private speculators—Mitchell/Giurgola have faithfully provided the civic client with a high normative level of building. In twenty-five years of practice they have consistently realized cultivated and effective environments conscientiously dedicated to the conduct of everyday life. It is significant that of the sixty-two buildings included in this volume over two-thirds have been designed for the public domain. In this sense, their practice has been exemplary, for they have suceeded, in a highly privatized epoch, to build responsibly for the needs of the society as a whole.

Notes

1. The shift towards the so called New Monumentality begins with the manifesto *Nine Points on Monumentality* written by Sigfried Giedion, José Luis Sert and Fernand Léger in 1943 while Giedion and Léger were living in the United States. This early recognition that modern architecture had become emotionally and symbolically inaccessible, reemerges in Paul Zucker's book *The New Architecture and City Planning* published in 1944 which was, in effect, the publication of a series of papers which had been given at a seminar held in 1944 at Columbia University. Kahn's earliest known theoretical text appears in this volume. Significantly enough this essay also deals with the theme of monumentality, with Kahn asserting that tectonic structure must be the prime key to the generation of modern monumental form.

2. R. Giurgola, Talk at the Curtis Institute of Music, Philadelphia, Pennsylvania, Commencement Day, 7 May 1976.

3. R. Giurgola, "Notes on Buildings and Their Parts," *The Harvard Architectural Review,* Spring 1981, p. 175.

4. R. Giurgola, "Architecture is both image and reality. . . ," *Space/Design,* December 1975, p. 3.

5. R. Giurgola, "Motivations to Architecture: An Introspection," unpublished essay, September 1975.

A REFLECTION

Ehrman B. Mitchell

In reflecting upon the twenty-five years of work since we first began our architectural firm, I think we have always sought to produce an architecture of consequence. In setting that goal for ourselves, we were aspiring to an architecture that could be judged on the basis of its consequence for human life. Consequence as the basis of judgment demands an equal and constant attention to the aesthetic, functional, symbolic and environmental aspects of each project. It seems to me that architecture worthy of this judgment arises from many determinants, but there are these two principal factors: the architect's working method and one's intentions as shaped by the openness and responsibility of one's mind to society at large.

The working methods leading to an architecture of quality demand a preoccupation with thoroughness, leaving no gaps in the process of designing and building. Wherever there are serious intentions, as in a design oriented firm, there must be an equal and serious attention to technology, management and building. There must be a continuing search for combinations of design and detailing, which simplify, reveal essentials and calibrate the hierarchy of building elements. This search fosters an emergence of fresh and diverse ideas in the firm's projects; it is a heartening sign, it indicates a quest for experiment, it veers from stereotype and stylistic tendencies; it seeks to invest each project with a sense of architecture as a personal act in terms of a strong response to human needs, to human scale and to a humane environment. Here the architectural intention is revealed.

From the beginning, we have clearly understood our architectural aim, our need to do important work, our need to complement each other through a commonality of goals and to hold a single purpose. It is this purpose that generates a natural process for its realization. An organizational set-up where lines of "pass and trespass" are defined gives way to establishing the pathways of convenience and professionalism. Those who have joined us from the beginning came as professionals dedicated to our purpose and our methods.

The central idea of the firm's work was and remains a process of making architecture that is propelled by design teams, one for each project. The design team leader and the other architects of the team commit their professionalism to their project from its inception to its completion, each remaining in a supporting role throughout. It is paramount that our design teams build that which they design and detail. This fosters a calibration of vision and realism. In our process, each of us contributes to a project's completion in differing ways and in varying degrees as needs dictate. We carry on the supporting administration and management of the firm as essential to achieving our purpose. Ours is a generalist approach in which every member of the firm plays many roles. This approach gives buoyancy to the development of our work, it serves us well, it remains even more important to meet the challenge of making architecture today.

Our methods are not without pitfalls. A constant renovation within the office is found by intentionally bringing young architects into our midst and taking them through this one team-one building process. Yet there is no easy alternative to the experience of a skilled architectural group which has worked together over a series of projects and has learned our methods and our intentions.

However, intermingling our groups with young and inexperienced architects fosters an enthusiasm for the pursuit of innovative thought that finds easy acceptance in our office. In this context we are always wary of the restraints imposed by regulatory agencies which can become barriers to our objectives. We are mindful of the burdens of over-experience that stifle experiment and intimidate a differing approach. We are watchful of the routine of repetition as it may hamper inventiveness. We constantly seek to renovate our professional group while still maintaining an experience which is nurtured by our goals and coalesces to mean teamwork in its best sense.

Thus, attempting to develop our working method engenders an openness of thought and harbors the discipline of facing new tasks. We seek an architecture which is not a series of unyielding, rigid relationships, but rather an environment which comes into being through its awareness of human strengths, requirements and desires. In our view, to aspire to an architecture of consequence demands revealing the way in which architects approach the making of a building, whether it be with thought or thoughtlessness, sensitivity or brashness, with an open mind or one dimmed by the trappings of preconceived notions.

These intentions reveal themselves not only in the work itself, but also in the activities surrounding the working process and contiguous to it. I am convinced that values accrue to individual architectural projects directly in proportion to the architect's commitment to engage in research and intensive study about each project. Further, these values emerge from initiatives to educate one's self thoroughly in history and humanities, and to devote time to a participation in academe, in professional development and in the specifics of the human dynamic. Each of us broadens our scope, furthers our insights and more fully prepares for the responsibility we have in our work for the people, for the cities and for the land. In turn, the quality of thought brought to the firm is enhanced and enriched. Through this evolving maturation a conviction firms, a sense of one's place and one's deeds is assured and one can marvel at the fabrications and fantasies of others whose constant battle is to say with erudition little of pertinence, less of fact and nothing of consequence.

From this architectural background, I became increasingly interested in projecting our experience and approaches to architecture into the profession as a whole. This pursuit brought me into our professional organization as an active participant. In every discipline which seeks to be considered as a profession by the public at large, the debate has centered on the ability and willingness of its members to be more than a protective association, to rise above the orientation of unionism. Dedicated members of a profession do not hesitate to attempt to take a stand, to be a shaping force within society, or to accept a responsibility for what is "now" and for what "will be." It is with this intensity of effort and with clear purposes understood by all that the benchmark of credibility with the public is established. A profession in one sense is merely a mechanism, like religious or social forms, out of which conventions for human behavior arise. These conventions may be cumbersome and introverted. The potential always exists that a profession may have the propensity to become self interested. In this case the public perceives it as a special interest group which possibly could be an adversary. In my view, it is critical that the profession remember that architecture comes before architects. As such, it is our responsibility to find the means to broaden public awareness of the visual built environment. Our country is nearly barren of the magnificient legacy of Western Europe, where every child matures with a conscious or unconscious awareness of a two thousand year tradition of shelters, constructions and architectural design which impinge upon one's life at every step. In that civilization there is a broad consciousness of architecture as an art which is substantially missing in our own. This broad awareness accepts architecture as a record of a culture, and its ultimate result is a society or public which makes architecture noble. The stimulation of this awareness of architecture within the public sector and the education of the young toward understanding both contemporary and historical architecture as a shaping force in society is the prime responsibility of our professional organization. We must lead now in order that we may follow later.

Thus, our years of work have taught us that producing an architecture of consequence must become the determination of each who participates with us. Its demands are personal to each architect, they extend to an intention, they are manifest in an attitude. The underpinning of professionalism is to achieve exemplary performance. It succeeds through an artful outreach to people, to the public. A profession establishes the public trust and fosters the public awareness of architecture. The public, in turn, joins the quest for quality and one day the quest for achieving an architecture of consequence.

CONSTANTS

Romaldo Giurgola

The ageless task of architecture has always been to produce an appropriate response to people's aspirations for a better life. In the pages which follow, buildings are illustrated which we hope will be perceived as responses in the spirit of those aspirations. We intend our architecture to be work in the context of art, dedicated to the resolution of the inherent contradictions in life and the balancing of opposite forces rather than the mere restatement of them. If society struggles at present amidst impinging and violent forces, that fact does not constitute a mandate for architects merely to imitate such disorder. Rather, the timeless aspiration for better lives stands as an eternal mandate, and suggests that buildings and places should be designed not only to tell "what we are" at this moment, but also should attempt to embody "what we ought to be" in the sense of being life-enhancing, to use an old-fashioned phrase.

In my view, architecture is not to be judged according to its consistency of style or its capacity to demonstrate an aesthetic or political polemic. Rather, each building should be evaluated separately according to its ability to acknowledge the variety of human pleasures, desires, needs and aesthetic concerns which are bound up in any project and to mould them gently into a true place. By the concept "place" we mean an architectural space which is rich enough in its amalgamation of individual parts to give free rein to the expression of individual functions and identities, yet at the same time which focuses that variety into a defined character which forms a unified whole.

During the past twenty-five years of our work, I have come to believe that to the extent to which "places" can be consciously or rationally formulated, this process occurs through the addressing of certain *constants* in one's architectural work. As an implicit working method, the continual attempt to address such constants in design is in no way equivalent to a search for a consistency of style. In the latter case it is "style" which supersedes each building and its particular demands, while in the former each building remains primary, and the constants embodied within its design are infinitely variable and malleable, being constant only in their existence as eternal elements related to concerns in human life. Although difficult to define, those constants which have occupied us over the years in the design of the work illustrated here may be said to be (1) the definition of a place through a sequence of rooms as constituent parts, (2) the language of space understood as an internal or external definition in the formulation of an itinerary, (3) resonance as an essential quality of architecture and (4) the development of an architectural aesthetic based upon a building's accessibility, clarity and power to elucidate its meaning and relationships.

The definition of a place in architecture is in fact the definition of the human measure for an activity, a deed or simply a presence, resulting in an adequate physical form in which each of these functions may unfold. It is from the architect's assessment of its parts that a building is primarily made: doorways, windows, floors and steps are all immediately perceivable at human scale and are built in relation to the measure of man. As an extension of the scale of those elements, rooms are the places formulated to contain or encourage human activities. We thus attempt to make our buildings as a sequence of rooms acquiring their measure not only through their role of evoking human activities or presences but also through their relative relationship to other elements of the environment. By contrast to this concept of sequential rooms, an all-encompassing "total view" in architecture seems to be something to which to aspire only as a general conceptual gesture rather than as something from which to begin, since most buildings would remain simple diagrams unless a conscious attitude had been determined toward their parts.

With respect to the second constant, the concept of rooms implies the concept of space, since the language of architecture is the language of space understood as an internal or external definition. It seems to me that good spaces are never the result of mere clever manipulations, since the language of space goes beyond time and stylistic tendencies. Space is either transformed into "true" architecture or it remains merely as a void; we have attempted to make this transformation take place in our work through the formulation of architectural itineraries among a building's spaces. These spatial linkages function as visual itineraries which are capable of comprehending, directing and accompanying a building's users in an atmosphere sympathetic to their actions.

This sense of spatial itinerary introduces the third constant, which seems to me to be the most essential quality of architecture. This is its "resonance," its capacity to link itself, whether visually or conceptually, with the long historical tradition of other buildings or places. Innovations introduced in architecture for the sake of contrivance or newness are against the concept of resonance, as they separate the building and its inhabitants from the rich associations of tradition and make them stand alone, harshly destitute of the collective memory of shapes, functions and meaning. At the foundation of architecture is a cultural tradition which has nothing to do with the random exploitation of the forms of the past. As a tradition it is more than a series of physical configurations; it is a series of "ways of seeing" and "ways of understanding" which constitute a major source of enrichment of our work and our lives.

The concept of an accessible cultural tradition leads to the fourth constant mentioned above, the development of an architectural aesthetic. In our own work, we have attempted to center this development upon two related ideas: first, that a building should respond both to the order of the city and the order of the land, and second, that the memory of a building's "beginning" should be expressed in its form. It has become increasingly clear throughout past years that built forms gain little by standing in harsh contradiction to the grand design of the natural environment. In the same way that the order of the city naturally varies in response to differences in land configuration, climate or orientation, the design for an individual building should also seek to establish a proper balance between surrounding elements of the natural and built environment. The search for this balance is central to the design process and is a determinant to which all other aesthetic, symbolic and functional considerations within the design must continually be related.

The expression of a memory of a building's "beginnings" is also central to formulation of an aesthetic. By "beginnings" I mean both the most basic conceptions from which a building grows—whether in the literal sense of a lintel resting upon two pillars or in the figurative sense of "shelter" in its most basic meaning—as well as the individual contributions made by the variety of people who shaped the design. In either case, what is expressed is a sense of explanation through which the building's aesthetic is based upon its accessibility, its clarity and on its power to elucidate its meaning and relationships rather than upon a calculated ambiguity.

In slowly exploring these four constants in our work we have continually realized their complexity. In the final analysis, an architect (as any artist) must simply strive to do "good" work. To have "beauty" as an obvious objective is merely to play to the galleries, and more often than not it constitutes a game which is unproductive of lasting values. Rather, it appears that all of us within the architectural profession face two primary tasks in the coming years. First, we must learn to design places and accommodations which have a more apparent significance for people's lives, whether at work or at home, and second, we must become more sensitive to individual human issues while at the same time working with unaccustomed dimensions.

The means by which an architect may rise to the challenge of those tasks is through the adherence to principles in his work. *Principles* in that sense are different from the *constants* already described above, although the presence and exploration of both elements in an architect's work is through conscious choice, not accident. Constants relate primarily to the physical solution found for a building, while principles serve as a guidance toward the way in which problems must be approached, interpreted and resolved. Principles are the values upon which judgments are made: they tell us in architec-

tural terms what is significant, what represents an example upon which to draw and what deserves to be a model. The intentional recognition of having principles as an architect is equivalent to being conscious of working for a purpose, which is one of architecture's most wonderful rewards for its practitioners.

Thus, we do not face these dual tasks in the future of architecture alone, for we face them above all with the aid of the past. Rather than using the past as a "grab-bag" from which the memory of a few details is occasionally extracted, we should realize that it stands as a quiet teacher deeply versed in an architecture of individual sensitivities within a grand scale. The architecture of the past always seems to be capable of planting the necessary seeds in our thoughts for the solution of our contemporary dilemmas. As in ancient Greece it is still possible to develop in architecture that symmetry existing between our forms and the forms of nature. It is a consistent symmetry in which architecture finds its measure not in conceptual abstractions but rather in the diversity of human aspirations, aspirations which are sensitive to the balance of nature and to the spirit of nature as the place of our beginning.

HQ Building, National Park Service
Acadia National Park
Bar Harbor, Maine. project 1967

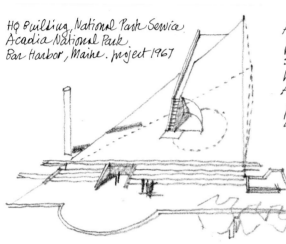

A site is the configuration of a place, a natural or artificial structure of which architecture must become an integral part. A place is the complex of human presences which includes architecture and the landscape.

Casa Thomas Jefferson
Brasilia, Brazil 1974

A meeting place is dependent upon the convergence of human pleasures, desires, and needs, of aesthetic concerns and principles, and of multiple relationships between the built and the natural, or between the land form and architectural form.

Newman Center
U. of Kentucky
Lexington, Ky.
project 1965

Swarthmore Presbyterian Church
Swarthmore, Pa. project 1965
↓

U.S. Embassy
Bogotá
Colombia
project 1968

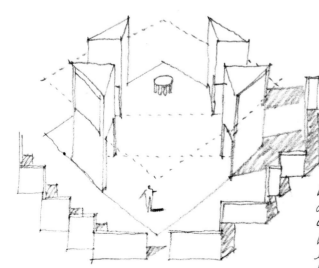

An emphasis on architectural elements produces the true focus of a meeting place: this focus arises from a confluence of light. Variations in the quality of light determine the character created for different meeting places — direct or diffuse, intense or casually dissipated, controlled or open to the influence of the environment outside the walls.

Worship Assembly Building
Benedictine Society of St. Bede
Peru, Illinois 1973

National AIA Headquarters building
Washington D.C. project 1967

WRIGHT BROTHERS MEMORIAL VISITOR CENTER
National Park Service
Kill Devil Hills, North Carolina 1960

The site of the Wright Brothers National Memorial is a flat, treeless, oceanfront plain bounded by dunes and punctuated by markers indicating the locations of the Wrights' pioneering experiments in powered flight. The visitor center contains an assembly room housing a replica of the first airplane, a museum, administrative offices, and a sunken terrace for lectures and ceremonies.

In order to be identifiable to visitors approaching in the flat terrain, the building is slightly elevated on a 128 foot square platform. Entirely constructed of poured-in-place concrete, the structure is a system of deep piers with bush-hammered surfaces and flat slabs which are designed to provide sun control for the glass walls which exhibit wide views of the historic site. The assembly room is roofed with a thin shell concrete dome with opposing thin shell overhangs. This roof structure spans 40 feet from column to column, allowing natural light into the display areas while also forming a strong exterior focal point compatible with the free forms of the nearby dunes.

1 View from the south
2 Assembly room
3 Ceiling detail
4 Site sketch

UNIVERSITY MUSEUM ACADEMIC WING
University of Pennsylvania
Philadelphia, Pennsylvania 1971

This five story addition to the University Museum is attached to a partially completed Lombardy Renaissance building of 1898. It houses a public education facility on its first two floors and the University of Pennsylvania's Departments of Anthropology and Archaeology above. Public facilities include a 100,000 volume library, lecture hall, restaurant and exhibition galleries.

Contrast has been used in the design of the addition to engage and stimulate the encounter between past and present, as the collection of the museum does. On the exterior the new construction is brought into close relationship with the existing museum by the use of the same dark red brick and tile as well as by regarding its mass, cornice height and roof pitch. The openings in the new brick walls provide a counterpoint to the existing structure with new contrasting large scale openings.

The addition completes the enclosure of one of the original courtyards and uses the captured outdoor space as a visual tool for clarifying the complexities of movement between the varying levels of the old and the new buildings. Two diagonal bridges and a transparent link structure containing lobbies and a restaurant cross the court to connect the buildings. A clear image of these new pedestrian routes and connections between the buildings is presented through the use of concrete for their construction, which is separate and distinct from the brick in color and texture.

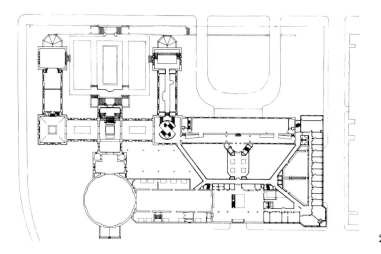

2

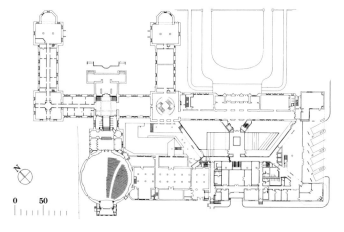

3

1

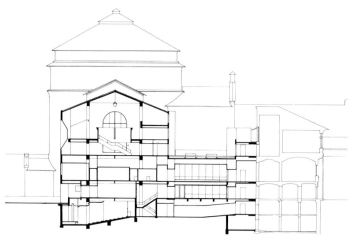

4

5

6

7

8

9

10

11

12

WORSHIP ASSEMBLY BUILDING
Benedictine Society of St. Bede
Peru, Illinois 1973

The original St. Bede Abbey Building encompassed a high school, refectory and monastery, each housed in separate wings of a nineteenth century structure located in a large open field. The Worship Assembly Building addition is intentionally placed as the focal point for the entire complex, and is viewed in front of and within the frame of the older buildings.

The Assembly's square central room is inserted diagonally into the U-shaped configuration of the existing building, with its triangular orientation structuring circulation through a series of skylit public and private passageways linking each major entry point. This plan allows for enlargement of the structure according to future needs with no disruption to the basic concept of the design.

Four large triangular light monitors, each 43 feet high and 20 feet on a side, project inward from the square sides of the room to bathe the interior in natural light. This simple luminosity within white walls devoid of ornament is appropriate to liturgical functions and to secular lectures for which the room is used.

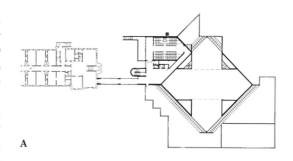

A

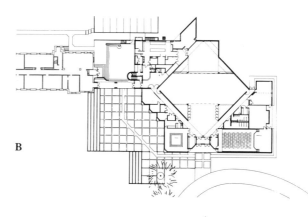

B

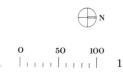

A) Second floor plan: *open to assembly room, choir* 1
chapel, bridge to monastery B) First floor plan: *assembly
room, chapels, conference rooms*
View from the southwest 2
View from existing monastery 3

2

4 Assembly room
5 Assembly room and skylit passageway
6 Main chapel from the northeast
7 Main chapel

8 Main entry

INDIAN POINT
ENERGY EDUCATION CENTER
Consolidated Edison Company of New York, Inc.
Buchanan, New York 1975

1

View from outdoor amphitheater 1
A) First floor plan: *upper exhibition space* B) Ground floor plan: *exhibition,* 2
simulator viewing, conference areas C) Basement floor plan: *offices,*
simulator, maintenance
Site sketch with generating station 3

The Indian Point electric power generating station is located 40 miles north of New York City on a hilly, 325 acre site overlooking the Hudson River. During the initial development and construction of the power plant, the surrounding forest was damaged, and the character of the natural landscape was radically altered. The function of the Energy Education Center project was threefold: to restore the surrounding land to a more natural state and to minimize the visual intrusion of the power plant on the landscape; to provide a facility to train personnel to operate the controls of a nuclear generating station; and to establish a visitors' center to house an exhibition illustrating the development of electrical energy and its impact upon the environment.

The training facility consists of classrooms, offices, a library and a special area which simulates the control room of the generating station. Exhibition spaces, an auditorium and a viewing area to observe the activity of the simulator are included in the visitors' center. An open-air walkway or promenade links parking areas to the Center, and will eventually extend to a concrete catwalk over the landscape as the grade drops off, terminating in a viewing platform above the power generator turbines. The two-level exhibition hall is integrated into this promenade and is flanked by a large circular clearing in the woods sown with wildflowers. The hall's glass roof and walls intentionally maintain a close visual connection for the visitor between explanatory displays inside and the surrounding plant and landscape beyond; this close proximity also encourages the viewer to complete his visit to the station with an exploration of the forest and nature trails encircling the site.

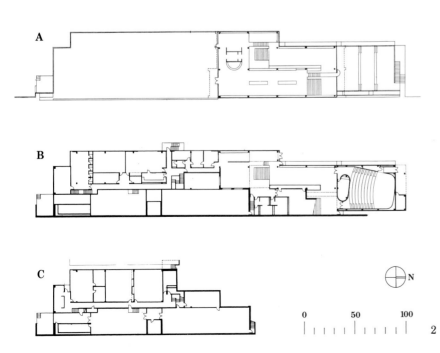

A

B

C

0   50   100

N

2

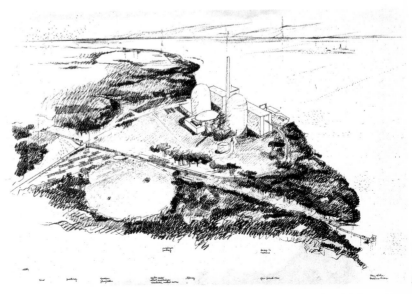

3

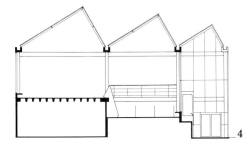

4 East-west section
5 Upper exhibition space
6 Exit to promenade
7 Section detail through west facade
8 Exhibition space

4

5

6

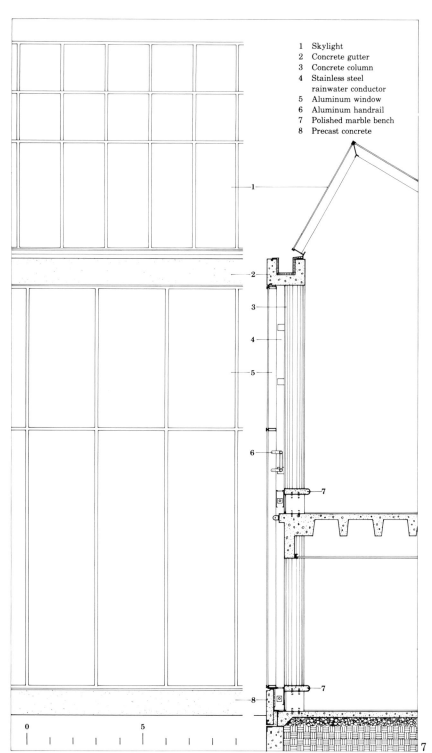

1 Skylight
2 Concrete gutter
3 Concrete column
4 Stainless steel
  rainwater conductor
5 Aluminum window
6 Aluminum handrail
7 Polished marble bench
8 Precast concrete

0   5

7

1

LIBERTY BELL PAVILION
National Park Service
Philadelphia, Pennsylvania 1975

1 North elevation
2 Site plan of Independence Mall
3 Ground level plan
4 East elevation

Shortly before the 1976 American bicentennial, it was decided to move the Liberty Bell from its location in Independence Hall in order to accommodate the huge crowds expected in Philadelphia. The new structure to house the bell would have to be capable of receiving and channeling great numbers of visitors with dignity, permitting the Bell to be viewed after hours and expressing its meaning without enshrinement.

The Liberty Bell pavilion, a long, narrow, low building on the axis of Independence Mall, is designed with glass walls on the north and south which allow an unobstructed view of Independence Hall to the north. Slightly ramped, broad brick terraces on three sides of the Pavilion offer easy access to visitors coming from all directions.

A narrow passage links the entrance vestibule on the north end with the Bell Chamber itself. This linear approach to the Liberty Bell takes place along the axis of Independence Hall rising in the background, an axial view which is emphasized by the skylight which illuminates the entire length of the passage. Upon reaching the Bell chamber, visitors listen to a short oral presentation, and exit through side doors onto flanking paved plazas.

Construction materials include white granite, a lead coated copper roof and oak interior paneling and floors.

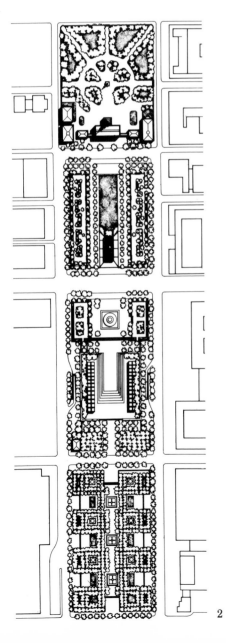

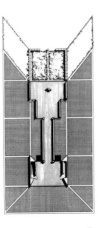

2

0   20   50   N   3

4

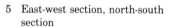

5 East-west section, north-south
   section
6 Entrance vestibule
7 East elevation
8 Bell chamber
9 South elevation
10 Liberty Bell
11 Independence Hall
12 Pavilion axis

CONCERT THEATER
C.W. Post Center, Long Island University
Greenvale, New York 1981

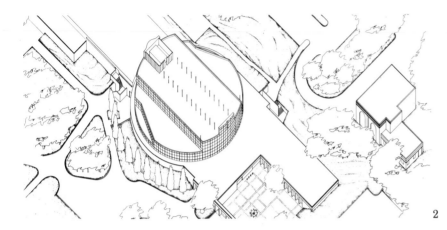

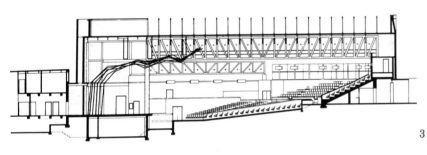

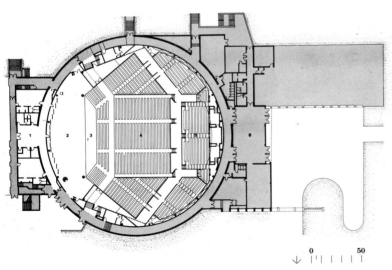

This concert theater was constructed within the preserved core of an assembly hall whose roof collapsed during a snow storm. It was rebuilt into a multipurpose performance hall seating 2250 people. Although the circular configuration of the original assembly hall was retained, the structure has been redesigned into a theater linearly oriented toward a large stage capable of accommodating full orchestras, dance troupes and other major performing groups. The building is composed of two basic elements: a "container" consisting of reinforced concrete walls, and a top "enclosure" formed by lightweight aluminum wall panels and a metal roof.

In the container, seating is carefully arranged in demarcated areas to foster a strong visual contact between performers and audience as well as a sense of intimacy and repose. At full capacity no spectator is more than 125 feet from the stage, and the distance from performer to viewer does not exceed 90 feet during dramatic performances. This arrangement of seating by contained areas also allows correction of the acoustical shortcomings of the inherited circular shape by means of angled walls and articulated surfaces. A system of sound reflecting "ribbons" radiating from the stage function as acoustical reflectors and provide hidden light sources and services to the stage from catwalks.

Interior surfaces are colored with shades from deep purple to red, while the aluminum wall panels and exposed roof structure are light grey and white. Outside the appearance of the original circular drum has been transformed into a series of longitudinal steps reflecting the structural configuration of the long spanning trusses. Red joint lines between wall panels, blue trim and runway lights atop the building contribute to the festive atmosphere of the theater.

1 View from the northwest
2 Axonometric
3 East-west section
4 Main floor plan: *1) dressing room, 2) stage, 3) pit and stage lift, 4) sloped seating, 5) tiered seating, 6) lobby*
5 Main entry

6 Assembly hall
7 Assembly hall
8 Section through stage
9 Acoustical ribbons

6

7

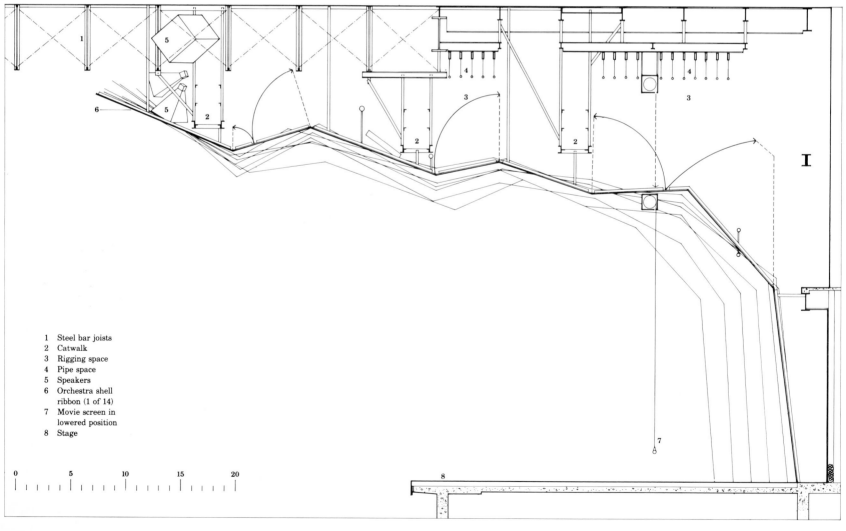

1 Steel bar joists
2 Catwalk
3 Rigging space
4 Pipe space
5 Speakers
6 Orchestra shell
  ribbon (1 of 14)
7 Movie screen in
  lowered position
8 Stage

0 5 10 15 20

8

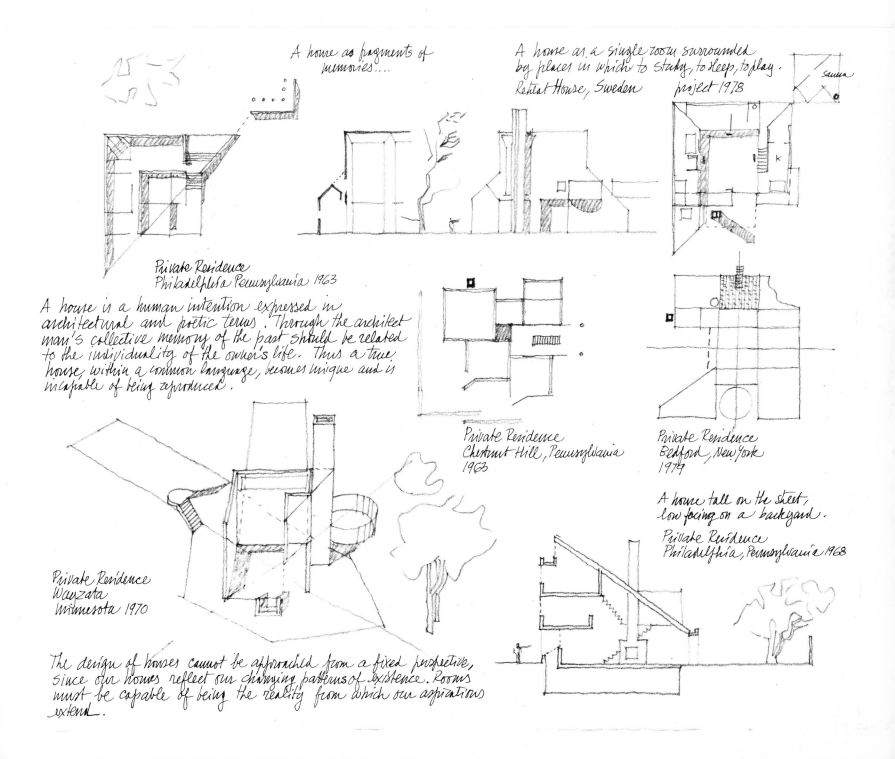

A house as fragments of
memories....

A house as a single room surrounded
by places in which to study, to sleep, to play.
Retreat House, Sweden   project 1978

sauna

Private Residence
Philadelphia Pennsylvania 1963

A house is a human intention expressed in
architectural and poetic terms. Through the architect
man's collective memory of the past should be related
to the individuality of the owner's life. Thus a true
house, within a common language, becomes unique and is
incapable of being reproduced.

Private Residence
Chestnut Hill, Pennsylvania
1963

Private Residence
Bedford, New York
1979

A house tall on the street,
low facing on a backyard.

Private Residence
Philadelphia, Pennsylvania 1968

Private Residence
Wayzata
Minnesota 1970

The design of houses cannot be approached from a fixed perspective,
since our houses reflect our changing patterns of existence. Rooms
must be capable of being the reality from which our aspirations
extend.

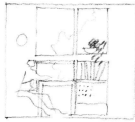
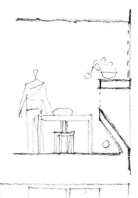

A student's house begins with a cell where a window means everything. It develops into an urban complex with meeting places, incorporating old buildings and forming new connections.

Undergraduate Housing
Yale University
New Haven, Connecticut
project 1975

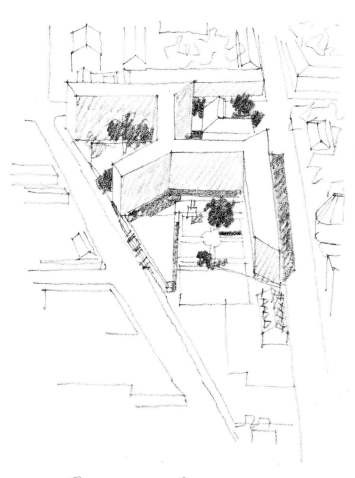

A high density city dwelling seeks relationships with natural elements and forms a linkage with existing architectural episodes.

Roosevelt Residential Development
Roosevelt Island, New York, N.Y.
project 1971

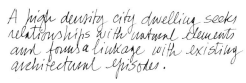

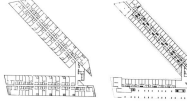

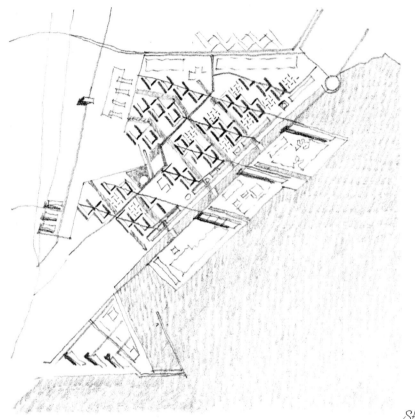

In multiple housing projects, a particular environment is developed which must always be conceived as being commensurate with liveability.
Its density is regulated by the need for mutual recognition among the inhabitants of the place.

Car traffic and walkways are separated but remain visible and integrated. In this project high rise apartments are placed near the open sea with distant views in all directions. Public buildings are aligned facing a quay.

City Redevelopment Plan
Tel Aviv, Israel competition, 1963

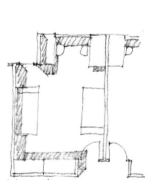

Mission Park Residential Housing. Williams College Williamstown Massachusetts 1972

Student Dormitory, Academy of the New Church, Bryn Athyn, Pennsylvania 1962

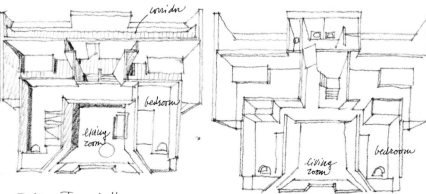

corridor
bedroom
living room
living room
bedroom

Each element of the building must be clearly perceived in itself as well in relation to the whole, since only by that means does the building elucidates its use, its scope, and its human measure.

International House
University of Pennsylvania, Philadelphia, Pennsylvania competition 1965

Wayzata, Minnesota 1970

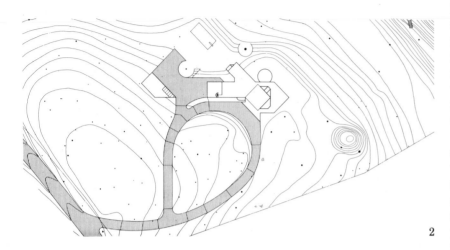

This house was designed for a family of four which included two young boys. The clients desired a single central area in the house which could accommodate large receptions while at the same time remaining intimate for the family. They also wanted views of the surrounding lush grounds and required that the bedrooms be placed in relatively separate areas. The sides of the site are diverse in character. The southern portion is dominated by a long sloping view of a lake framed by an Indian burial mound and several large trees. To the east the site slopes steeply toward the lake.

The various elements of the house are located in response to these site conditions. The elements originate from and wrap around a central double-height living room. The front walls of this room consist of a perforated elevation which filters the light entering the room and opens its spaces to a view of the lake and burial mound. The layer of secondary spaces surrounding this central area accommodates large parties, while maintaining a relatively small scale for the living room itself. The entry vestibule, garage and the service elements protect the privacy of the living room and other family areas of the house from the more public side of the site. The circular dining room, oriented to views of the grounds, extends from the living room gallery into a space sheltered and defined by the bedroom and kitchen wing. On the second floor of that wing, the bedrooms are oriented toward the east with its morning sun and panoramic views of the lake.

The house is of wood frame construction, with exterior walls of white painted vertical cypress siding and interior walls and ceilings of hard plaster.

1 East elevation
2 Site plan
3 Second floor plan: *1) master bedroom, 2) master bathroom, 3) sitting room, 4) roof terrace, 5) office, 6) bedroom, 7) bedroom, 8) laundry, 9) bedroom, 10) roof terrace*
4 First floor plan: *1) entrance gallery, 2) living room, 3) terrace, 4) dining room, 5) bar, 6) kitchen, 7) china store, 8) pantry, 9) recreation room, 10) guest powder room, 11) toilet, 12) wine cellar, 13) mud room, 14) garage*

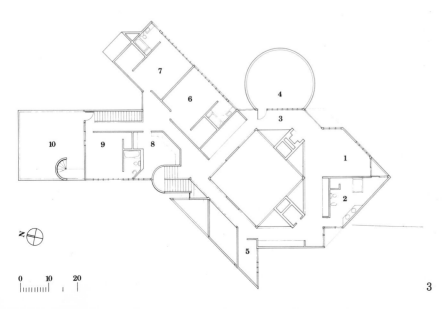

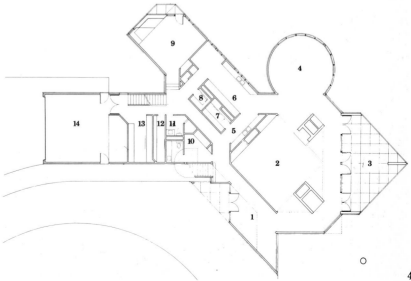

5

6

7

5 View of dining room from the southwest
6 Main staircase
7 Living room
8 West elevation
9 Dining room
10 Entrance, west elevation

8

9

10

1

2

Southwest elevation 1
View from the west 2
East elevation with main entry 3
West elevation with porch addition 4
View from the north 5

3

4

5

Conestoga, Pennsylvania 1979

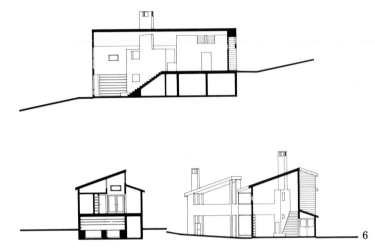

 6

 7

This house was designed for a family of four: a college professor, a stock broker and their two young sons. The family has informal living habits and requested an open relationship between living, dining and kitchen areas. Budget limitations required a program of phased design and construction in which the master bedroom initially occupied the area which became the children's playroom after a second phase addition.

Views of the beautiful hills and farmland from southeast to southwest are the major advantages of the site. The plan of the house is direct: living spaces on the lower level, sleeping areas above. Both levels have immediate access to the outside due to the sloping hillside. The windows take advantage of the views, to admit morning sun and to limit the entry of the afternoon sun. The house was built by Amish builders with conventional local materials: red painted wood clapboard siding over wood frame, standard operable wood windows and doors and grey asphalt shingle roofing. It is a house made by conventional means, but one which nevertheless becomes a special place responding to the family's lifestyle, phased construction plans, unshaded site and modest budget.

Sections 6
Study model 7
Lower floor plan: *1) living room, 2) dining* 8
room, 3) kitchen/pantry, 4) mud room,
5) storage, 6) future expansion, 7) terrace
Upper floor plan: *8) bedroom, 9) master*
bedroom, 10) screened porch

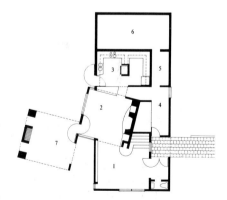

0   10   20   30   40   50

8

9

10

9 Living room from the master bedroom
10 Dining room from the living room
11 Southwest elevation with porch addition

NEWMAN RESIDENCE
Bedford, New York 1979

This house was designed for a family of five, although the family's three children attend college and are at home only for limited periods. The family required a central living space for communal activities and separate bedroom and service areas for greater privacy. In addition, they wanted the bedrooms to take advantage of the spectacular views.

The house is located at the edge of a field which slopes sharply down on two sides to a river gorge. The plan of the house is formed by a center double-height living area, flanked by bedroom pavilions on the view side of the site and by the service wing on the opposite side. Courtyards, each with its own character, separate the bedroom pavilions from each other and from the service wing, create a place of entry, and frame views to the river gorge and hills beyond. Varied ceiling heights and room configurations with differing qualities of light provide intimate and spacious places and accommodate a broad range of activities.

The house is built of wood stud construction with integral colored stucco exterior walls. A cedar shingled roof, sloping down from a high point above the central living room, unifies the exterior of the house.

1

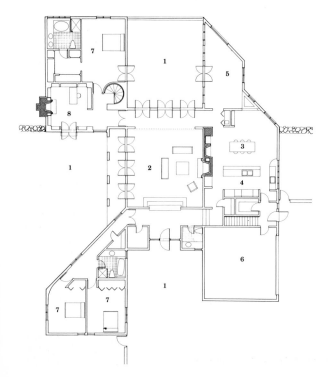

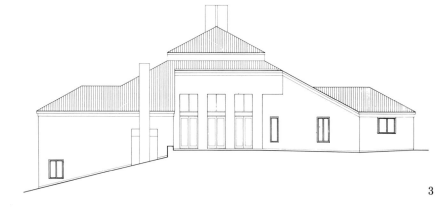

3

N

0   10   20
2

1 Study model
2 First floor plan: *1) court, 2) living room, 3) dining room, 4) kitchen, 5) plant room, 6) garage, 7) bedroom, 8) library*
3 South elevation
4 Entry court
5 Living room
6 View from the southeast

4

5

6

1

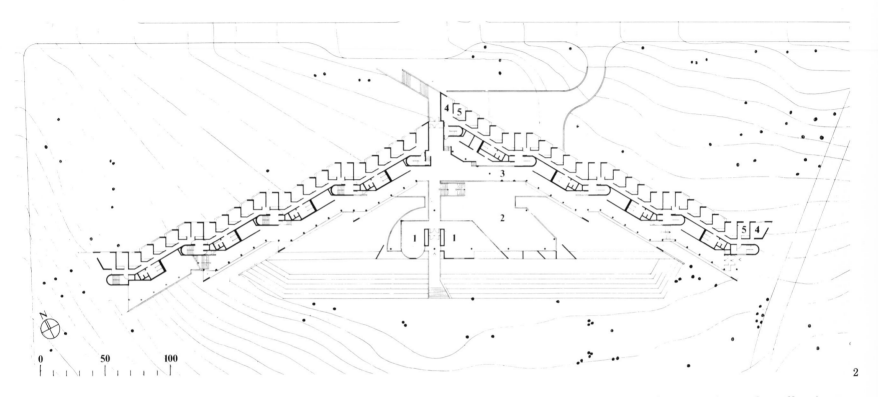

2

1 View from the south
2 First floor plan: *1) lounge, 2) dining room below, 3) gallery, 4) living room, 5) study-bedroom*
3 Early study model
4 Axonometric

3

This residential facility for 294 students continues the college's emphasis upon use of a suite system for all dormitories, in which each group living space is composed of several private study-bedrooms with a common living room and bathroom. Suites are grouped into four clusters, each containing approximately 75 students. The clusters share a dining hall, kitchen facilities, lounges, recreation rooms and laundries.

Located in the northeast segment of the campus, the building intentionally creates an enclosure for a neighboring park while not obstructing views of the distant Vermont mountains. Within the building, each study-bedroom is articulated as an individual unit and is provided with a large bay window which relieves the small size of the room. Four floors of suites are grouped between stairs which lead to the public gallery on the first floor. Each cluster of suites is offset progressively from the midpoint of the building to provide a separate identity for the cluster. This undulation of the building's form also intensifies the implied closure at the sides of the park, and allows an articulation of the exterior surface of the building.

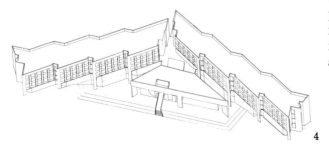

4

10

5 View from the west
6 Bridge to lounges
7 Central staircase
8 Dining room
9 Gallery
10 Southwest elevation

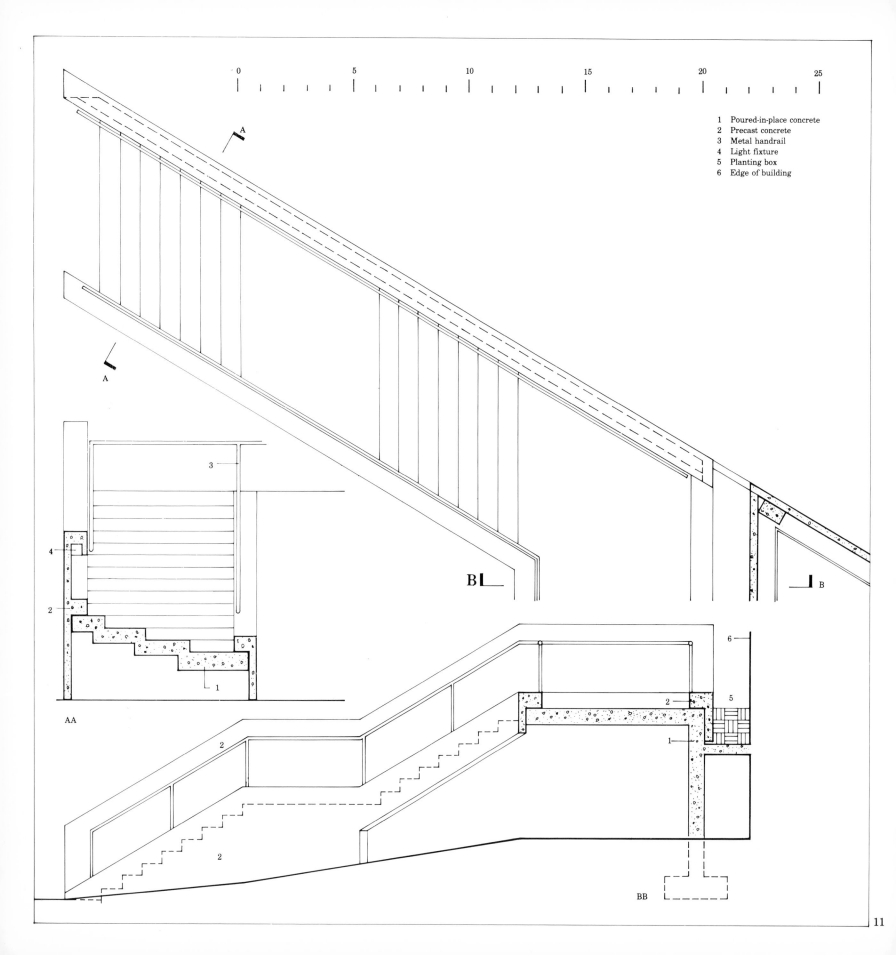

1   Poured-in-place concrete
2   Precast concrete
3   Metal handrail
4   Light fixture
5   Planting box
6   Edge of building

0   5   10   15   20   25

A

A

B

B

AA

BB

11

12

11 Entry staircase details
12 North elevation

BENI STABILI COMPETITION
Beni Stabili U.S.A., Inc.
Houston, Texas 1979

The design proposed the development of a two-block area north of Hermann Park in Houston into a complex containing two high-rise apartment buildings, an L-shaped group of terrace apartments and adjacent commercial space for shops and offices. The design seeks to create a lively urban space composed of individual family dwellings juxtaposed with spaces common to all residents. The configuration of the spaces maintains many of the qualities associated with family life in detached houses (i.e. privacy, views, spaciousness and neighborliness) and provides efficiency common to multifamily dwellings.

The shape of the terrace apartment building allows the maximum number of apartments to have prime views. The apartment tower design is organized around a central core, with entry to the apartments on alternate axes on every other floor. Each corridor terminates in an expansive, double-height galleria with a large window providing dramatic views into the landscape. By this means the arrival area on each floor is compact while remaining visually expansive.

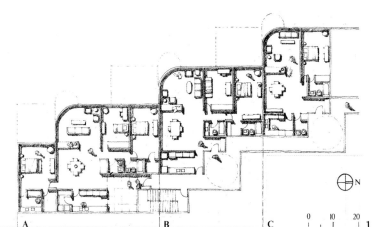

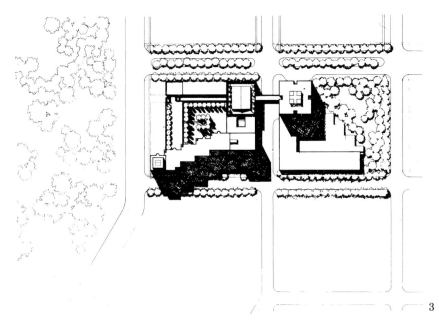

1 Unit plans of terrace apartments: *A) three bedroom unit, B) two bedroom unit, C) one bedroom unit*
2 Project sketch from the west
3 Site plan
4 Project model from the northwest

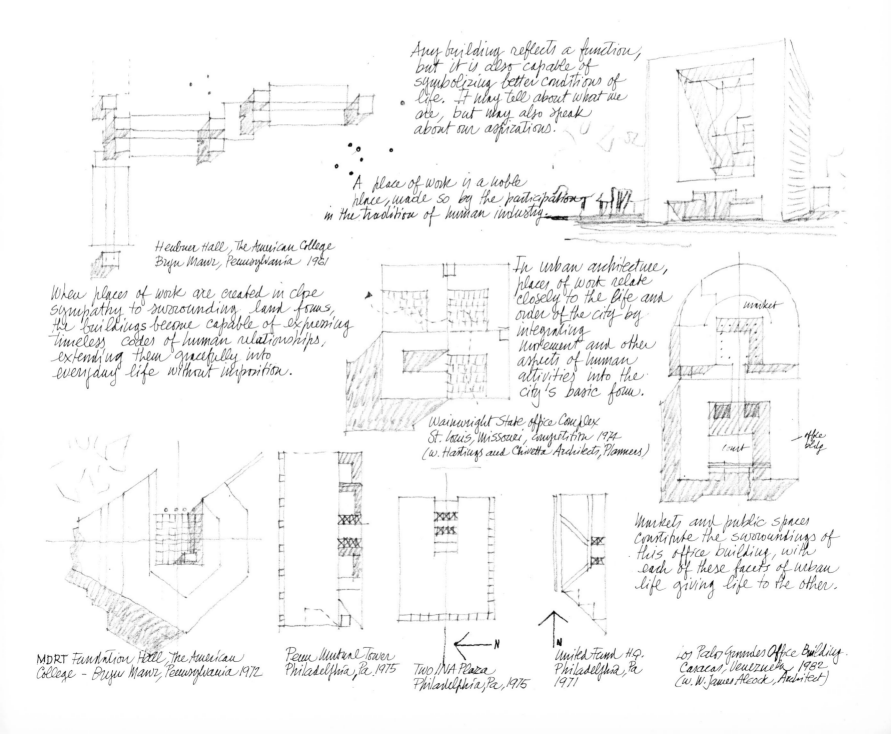

Any building reflects a function, but it is also capable of symbolizing better conditions of life. It may tell about what we are, but may also speak about our aspirations.

A place of work is a noble place, made so by the participation in the tradition of human industry.

Heubner Hall, The American College Bryn Mawr, Pennsylvania 1961

When places of work are created in close sympathy to surrounding land forms, the buildings become capable of expressing timeless codes of human relationships, extending them gracefully into everyday life without imposition.

In urban architecture, places of work relate closely to the life and order of the city by integrating movement and other aspects of human activities into the city's basic form.

Wainwright State Office Complex St. Louis, Missouri, competition 1974 (w. Hastings and Chivetta Architects, Planners)

market

office bldg

court

Markets and public spaces constitute the surroundings of this office building, with each of these facets of urban life giving life to the other.

MDRT Foundation Hall, The American College - Bryn Mawr, Pennsylvania 1972

Penn Mutual Tower Philadelphia, Pa. 1975

Two INA Plaza Philadelphia, Pa. 1975

N

United Fund H.Q. Philadelphia, Pa 1971

N

Los Palos Grandes Office Building. Caracas, Venezuela 1982 (w. James Alcock, Architect)

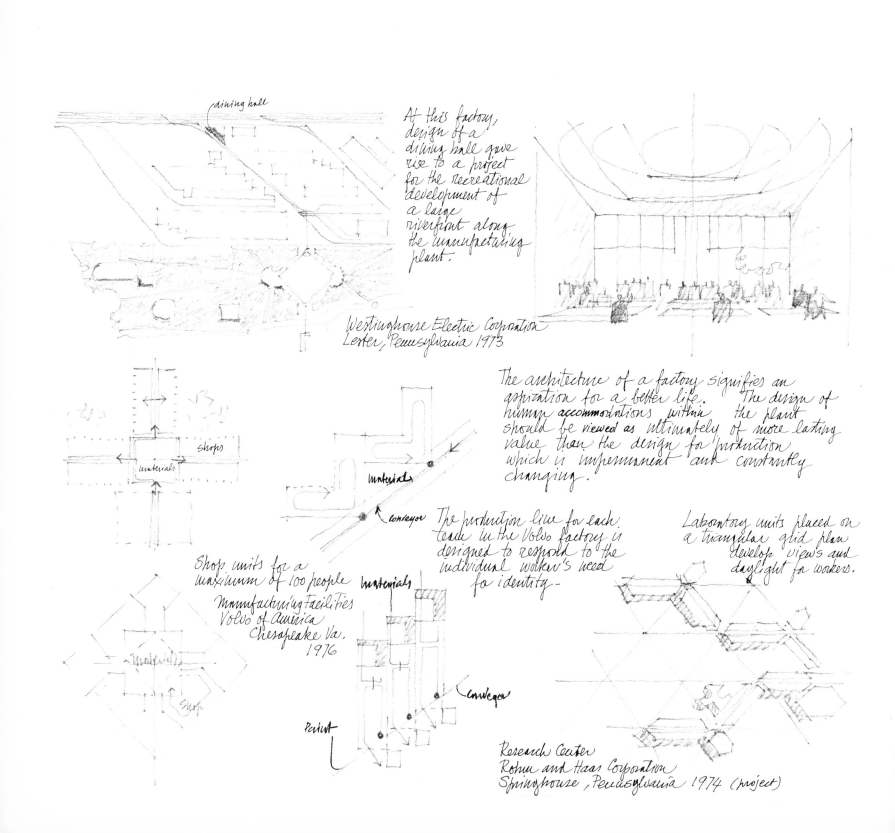

dining hall

At this factory, design of a dining hall gave rise to a project for the recreational development of a large riverfront along the manufacturing plant.

Westinghouse Electric Corporation
Lester, Pennsylvania 1973

The architecture of a factory signifies an aspiration for a better life. The design of human accommodations within the plant should be viewed as ultimately of more lasting value than the design for production which is impermanent and constantly changing.

shops

materials

materials

conveyor

The production line for each team in the Volvo factory is designed to respond to the individual worker's need for identity.

Laboratory units placed on a triangular grid plan develop views and daylight for workers.

Shop units for a maximum of 100 people

Manufacturing Facilities
Volvo of America
Chesapeake Va.
1976

materials

conveyor

shop

Product

Research Center
Rohm and Haas Corporation
Springhouse, Pennsylvania 1974 (project)

OFFICE BUILDING ADDITION
Philadelphia Life Insurance Company
Philadelphia, Pennsylvania 1962

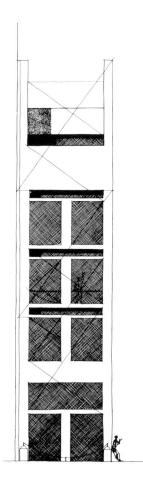

1 Street elevation
1 2 Elevation sketch

THE SCHECHTER GROUP BUILDING
The Schechter Group
New York, New York 1982

The designs of these two buildings, completed 20 years apart, address the same problem: to create a small scale urban structure capable of working with existing adjacent buildings to maintain the scale and inherent rhythm of the street while responding to particular programmatic demands for function and airiness within. The Office Building Addition provides loft type space on six floors congruent with the levels of the existing main building. While concrete for the addition's facade provides a new and contrasting vitality in juxtaposition to older surrounding buildings, the facade openings for the new building are intimately related to the Renaissance symmetry of the adjacent structures.

The Schechter Group building design is a renovation of a townhouse on a landmark block in Manhattan to house a communications design firm. Programming of the interior spaces focusses upon organizing floor plans to take maximum advantage of the limited natural light at the end walls. The new facade of the townhouse attempts to restore a sense of order to the rhythm of building widths on the block by forming a strong planar facade of grey limestone with a gridded texture and punched openings.

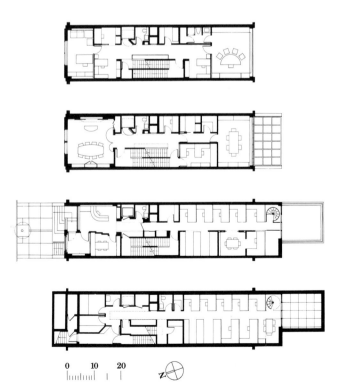

0   10   20

1

2

1 Floor plans
2 Model facade

UNITED WAY HEADQUARTERS BUILDING

United Way of Southeastern Pennsylvania
Philadelphia, Pennsylvania 1971

The site for this building is open on three sides to major urban views and adjoins a small scale residential and office area on the fourth. The headquarters provide office space and meeting rooms for the divergent departments. Six office floors are located above the public meeting rooms on the ground floor, a penthouse and roof deck houses the staff's dining room, lounges and recreation area.

The building is composed as a glass box surrounded by concrete sunscreens where needed. A different design solution was used for each facade according to its orientation. The glass curtain wall forming the north elevation allows floor-to-ceiling views of the cathedral across the street. The western wall consists of a brise-soleil of deeply recessed longitudinal openings which shade the glass and also house the perimeter air ducts. The large scale elements of this facade allow the building to be easily identified by the fast-moving traffic on the adjacent Parkway. The southwest elevation, parallel to the Parkway, has deep openings which respond to the main orientation of the building and provide space for the executive offices.

The interior layout of the office floors is based on a three-foot module which governs the partitions, window mullions, light fixtures and metal ceiling panels. The energy used for lighting provides much of the heat for the building which results in lower operating costs. Exposed poured-in-place concrete is used structurally and as a finished surface. Exterior walls are grey glass, set in dark grey anodized aluminum mullions.

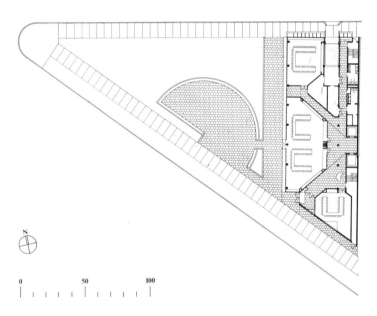

3

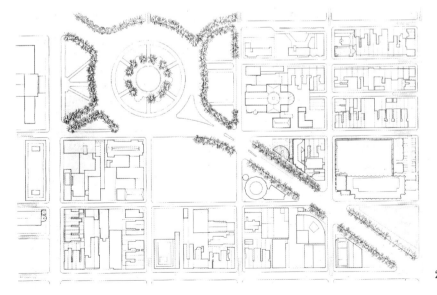

2

4

1 West elevation
2 Site plan
3 Ground floor plan: *reception and conference rooms*
4 South elevation

5

6

7

1 Poured-in-place concrete
2 Aluminum window
3 Air supply plenum
4 Return air plenum
5 Heat recovery light fixtures
6 Continuous air slot

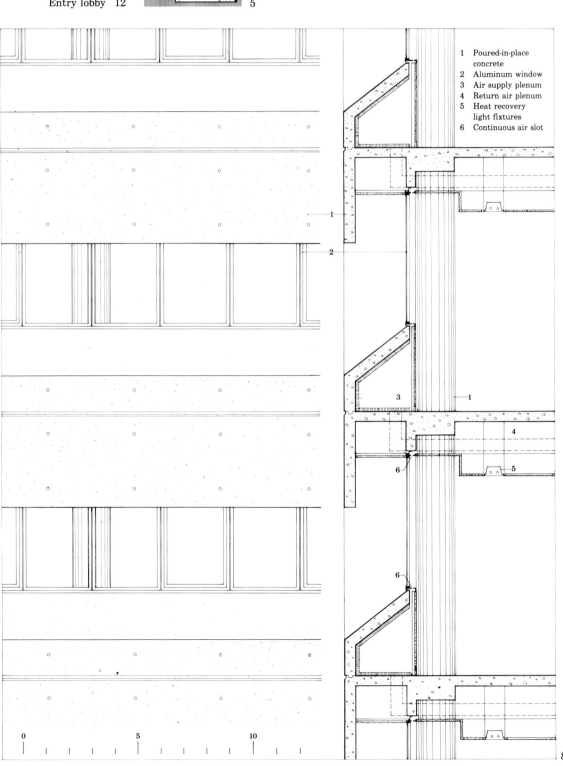

0   5   10

8

9

10

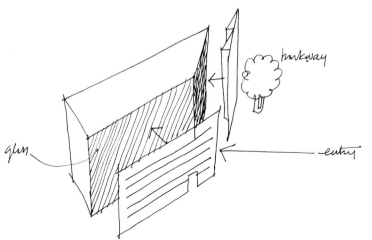

11

12

TWO INA PLAZA
Insurance Company of North America
Philadelphia, Pennsylvania 1975

Study model showing north facade 1
Section 2
Plan A: *typical office floor plan* 3
Plan B: *ground floor plan*
Street view of north elevation 4

1

The site for this 27 story tower is immediately west of the original INA Corporate Headquarters in the center of the city. Although adjacent to the existing headquarters, this project was designed as a separate building and covers the entire site. The ground floor has limited commercial areas with a public escalator connection to the train station concourse. The structural system is clear span steel from core to exterior wall with four rows of columns on a 30 foot spacing in the east/west direction. The skin of the building is made up of enameled formed aluminum panels and window mullions.

The building elevations are designed to respond to their differing orientations. The upper part of the east and south elevations and the entire west elevation consist of deeply recessed longitudinal openings with curved spandrels which function as solar deflectors. The spandrels also form the enclosure for the air conditioning and heating induction units. The lower portion of the south elevation is shaded by the adjacent building and the north elevation is entirely of glass since it receives no heat build up during working hours. The lower portion of the east wall is a party wall and serves as the utility core of the office tower.

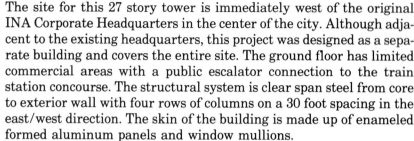

A

B

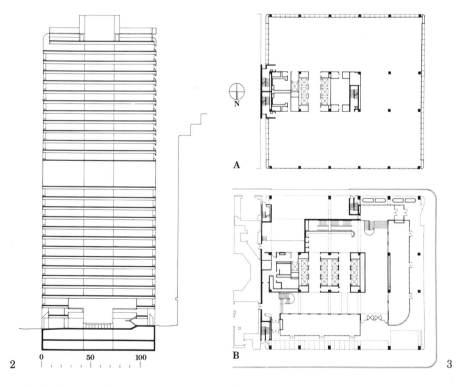

2

0   50   100

3

4

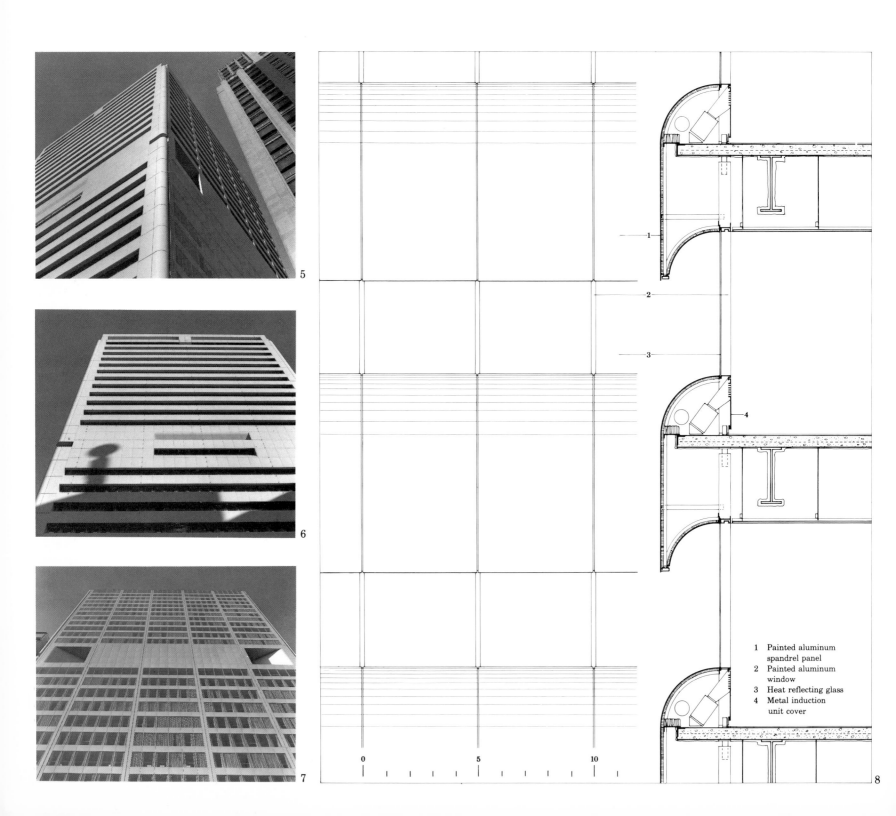

1 Painted aluminum
  spandrel panel
2 Painted aluminum
  window
3 Heat reflecting glass
4 Metal induction
  unit cover

0   5   10

5

6

7

8

9

10

PENN MUTUAL TOWER
Penn Mutual Life Insurance Company
Philadelphia, Pennsylvania 1975

This office building is a 449,000 square foot addition to the existing Penn Mutual complex in the center of the historic district in Philadelphia. The mass of the new building complements the existing structure and completes a symmetrical backdrop for Independence Hall on the axis of the Mall. The facade of a significant Egyptian Revival building originally located on the site was retained at street level in order to maintain a human scale for pedestrians. This facade, designed by John Havilland in 1835, is preserved as a four-story, freestanding sculpture defining the new building's entrance plaza. Glass enclosed elevators allow visitors to the historic area to ascend from the building's entrance plaza to an observation level on the top floor overlooking Independence Hall and the city. The generous floor-to-floor heights of the existing building are maintained in the new structure in order to provide direct connections. The modular east wall is poured-in-place concrete, which also acts as a sun screen on this broad exposure.

1

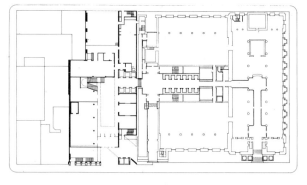

2

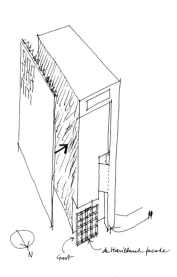

3

4

View from the north 1
Entry elevation 2
Conceptual sketch 3
First floor plan 4
Elevation sketch 5

6

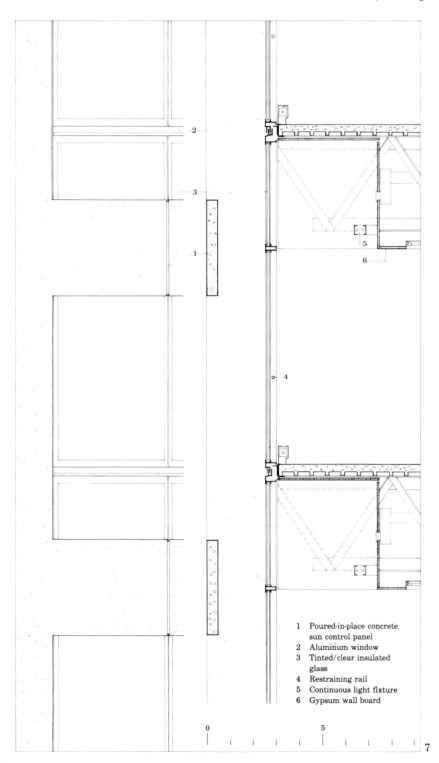

1 Poured-in-place concrete sun control panel
2 Aluminum window
3 Tinted/clear insulated glass
4 Restraining rail
5 Continuous light fixture
6 Gypsum wall board

0   5

7

8

THE PENNSYLVANIA
FIRE INSURANCE COMPANY

9

10

11

WAINWRIGHT STATE OFFICE COMPLEX
State of Missouri
St. Louis, Missouri 1981
With Hasting + Chivetta, Architects, Planners

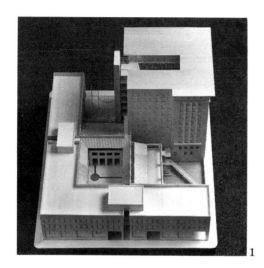

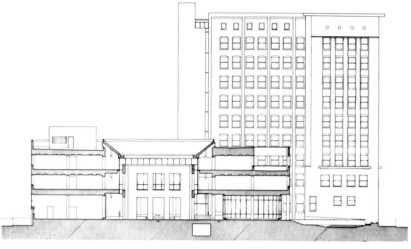

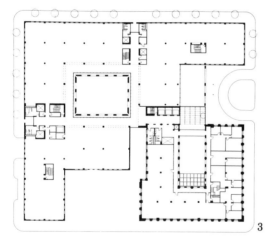

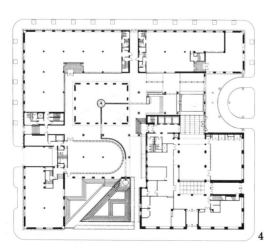

The Wainwright complex was the winning design in a national competition held by the State of Missouri for renovation of Louis Sullivan's Wainwright Building and construction of additional office space on the remainder of the city block in downtown St. Louis. The design consists of reuse of the original building in concert with the addition of three L-shaped low buildings unified by courtyards and plazas. The public nature of the building's program determined the basic form for the new addition. Retaining the original St. Louis quadrant division of the block, the complex has entrances on all sides, welcoming the public and facilitating pedestrian movement.

In the renovation of Sullivan's building, a central atrium was created by enclosing the original light well with a glass wall and roof and removing the windows from the light well walls. The atrium is closed on the north end with a ten-story window wall and bridges connecting each floor, allowing access to elevators relocated in a tower structure at the juncture of the old and new buildings.

The plazas and courtyards form a continuous transition between the old and new buildings. The east courtyard, open to the street, is formal with a fountain, while the second courtyard is secluded in character enlivened by a granite flume with running water. The third plaza, open to the street, is sculptured with flowerbeds and a triangular pool receiving water from the granite water-course. These spaces provide places for walking and gathering, and function as an urban area offering a number of choices for the user—places in the shade, in the sunlight or near the water.

N

50　　　0

1 Study model
2 Section looking east
3 Second floor plan
4 Ground floor plan
5 Courtyard

5

6

7

8

9

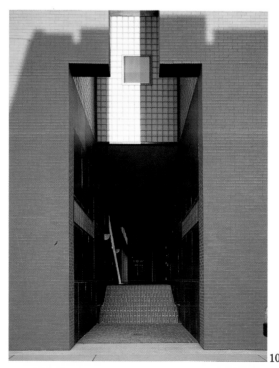

10

11

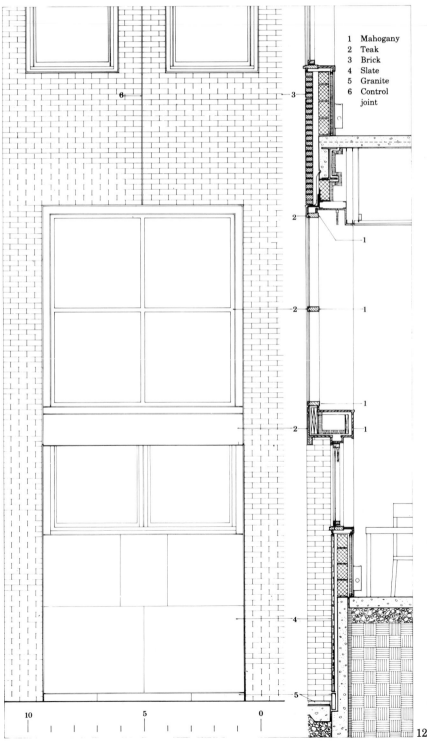

1	Mahogany
2	Teak
3	Brick
4	Slate
5	Granite
6	Control joint

13

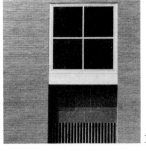

12

14

6 South plaza
7 View towards courtyard from the east plaza
8 Street view from the west
9 Atrium bridges
10 West entry
11 Detail of west facade
12 Section detail through west facade
13 East plaza
14 Detail of west facade

1

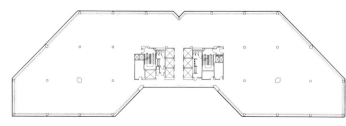

2

0 30 60 90

3

TEN STAMFORD FORUM
F.D. Rich Company
Stamford New Urban Corporation Subsidary
Stamford, Connecticut 1979

The design of this office building is determined by its particular location on a linear urban renewal site. Although controlled by a single developer, the site will eventually be occupied by four office buildings designed by different architects but unified by a common parking base surmounted by landscaped plazas. The Ten Stamford Forum project was the first of these buildings. It occupies the easternmost portion of the site in a position visible from the major expressway to the south.

The building is designed as a long, narrow rectangle with truncated corners, forming a visual gateway to the remainder of the complex. A large niche is carved out of the wide eastern facade to create a monumentally scaled portal. The niche provides natural light and visibility to the outdoors from the interior elevator lobbies, which are also the focal points for movement within the building.

In addition to creating a welcoming gateway to the complex, the configuration of the building also responds to other site conditions: the splaying of the short facades sharply reduces the number of offices which face the expressway directly, thus minimizing noise problems. Exterior surfaces of white marble and glass are carefully articulated. Particular attention is given to the problem of energy conservation by utilization of heat pumps and rooftop solar panels.

1 North elevation
2 Floor plan levels ten and eleven
3 Floor plan levels one through nine
4 Main entry
5 Site plan
6 North-south section

4

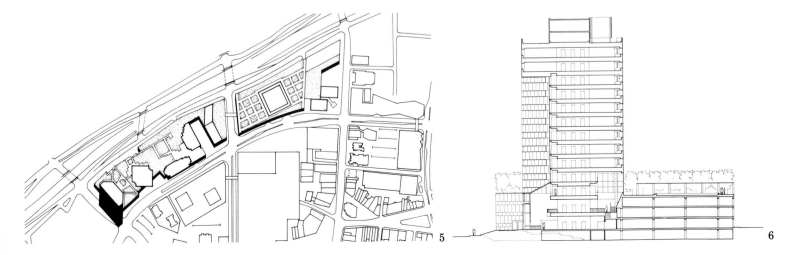

5

6

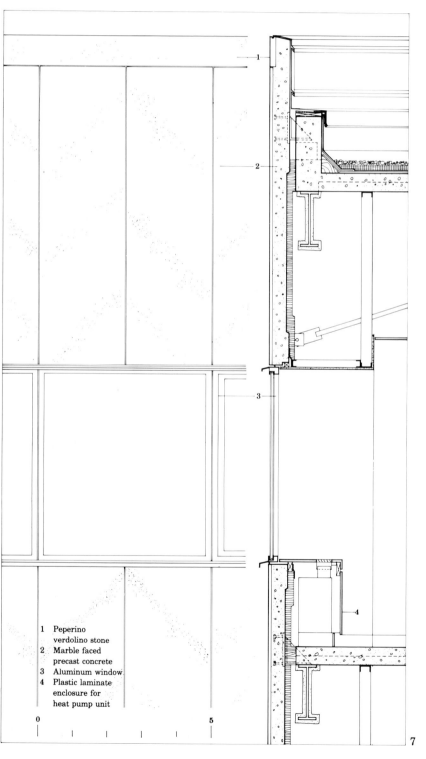

1 Peperino
   verdolino stone
2 Marble faced
   precast concrete
3 Aluminum window
4 Plastic laminate
   enclosure for
   heat pump unit

0   5

7

8

9

7 Section detail
through
exterior wall
8 Main entry
9 Lobby garden
10 View from the
northwest

10

ADMINISTRATIVE RESOURCES CENTER
Lukens Steel Company
Coatesville, Pennsylvania 1979

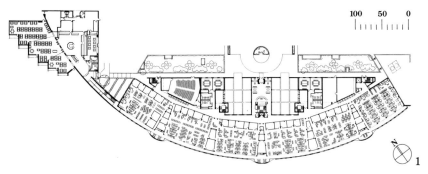

100 50 0

The Administrative Resources Center houses a number of administrative facilities previously scattered in different locations within the small town in which the steel plant is located. The decision to consolidate the administrative sector in a new headquarters building influenced the character of the architecture: the building symbolically functions as a bridge between the labor and management sectors of the plant. As a result, the site on a promontory was intentionally chosen to provide the administrative sector with panoramic views of the steel plant and its sequence of operations.

The building consists of three levels divided into open office bays, each containing approximately 50 people. The bays are distributed radially in an arc around two entrance courtyards for employees. The main lobby and formal entrance for visitors lies between the two courts. On the south side of the bays is a curvilinear wall of red brick and glass, repeating the red brick characteristic of small Pennsylvania towns. The wide windows along this wall provide ample natural light and views into the landscape for each office. The corridor following the wall's curvature serves as a circulation spine leading to the cafeteria building.

On the north side of the complex, the two entrance courts define more axes for conference rooms, the board room, special offices and services. In contrast to the red brick of the south facade, the northern wall elevations are faced with white glazed brick, and present a modestly scaled two-story facade commensurate with the clapboard houses surrounding the plant's perimeter.

Second floor plan: *offices and dining facilities* 1
Site model 2
Study model showing entry and office areas 3
View from west with dining facilities in foreground 4

5 South elevation
6 Office corridor
7 Interior staircase
8 Interior staircase
9 Dining room soffit detail
10 Dining room
11 Detail view of dining room

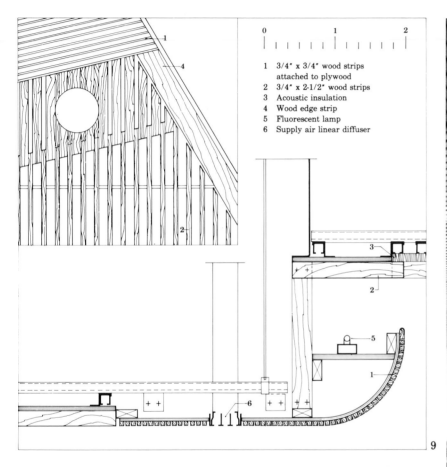

1. 3/4″ x 3/4″ wood strips attached to plywood
2. 3/4″ x 2-1/2″ wood strips
3. Acoustic insulation
4. Wood edge strip
5. Fluorescent lamp
6. Supply air linear diffuser

9

10

11

12

13

14

WILSHIRE-GLENDON OFFICE BUILDING
Wilshire-Glendon Associates, Ltd.
Los Angeles, California 1985
With Daniel, Mann, Johnson & Mendenhall

The design for this office/retail building originates within the split identity of its site, located upon Wilshire Boulevard, a major thoroughfare bordered by high density development, and the edge of Westwood Village, a treasured pedestrian scale community unique in Los Angeles. The paired masonry facades of the building give it a solid presence and function as a beacon from distant views. These nearly symmetrical walls also frame the smaller scale portion of the project which opens sympathetically into Westwood Village.

The form of the design draws upon precedents of internal shopping streets which evolved throughout the development of Westwood. The complex is entered from the west through a skylit shopping arcade which leads to an open square linking the retail portion of the project and the office tower. A boulevard-scaled entry also opens onto the courtyard which is insulated from the intense street activity. Exterior store frontage reinforces the differing character of each of the adjacent streets. The building's exterior color is determined by the warm rose hues of pink granite cladding. The courtyard and arcade create a contemporary oasis compatible with the traditional architecture of Westwood.

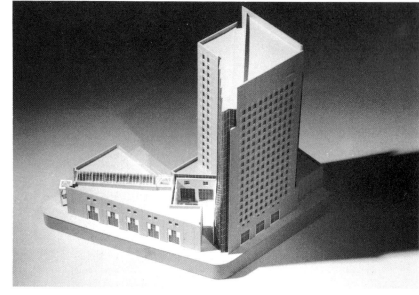

2

1

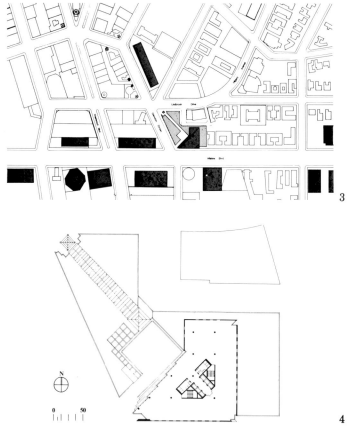

3

4

0   50

95

1 Sketch from the north
2 Model view from the west
3 Site plan
4 Typical tower plan
5 Sketch of Wilshire Boulevard facade
6 West elevation
7 Model view from the north
8 Courtyard sketch

5

6

7

8

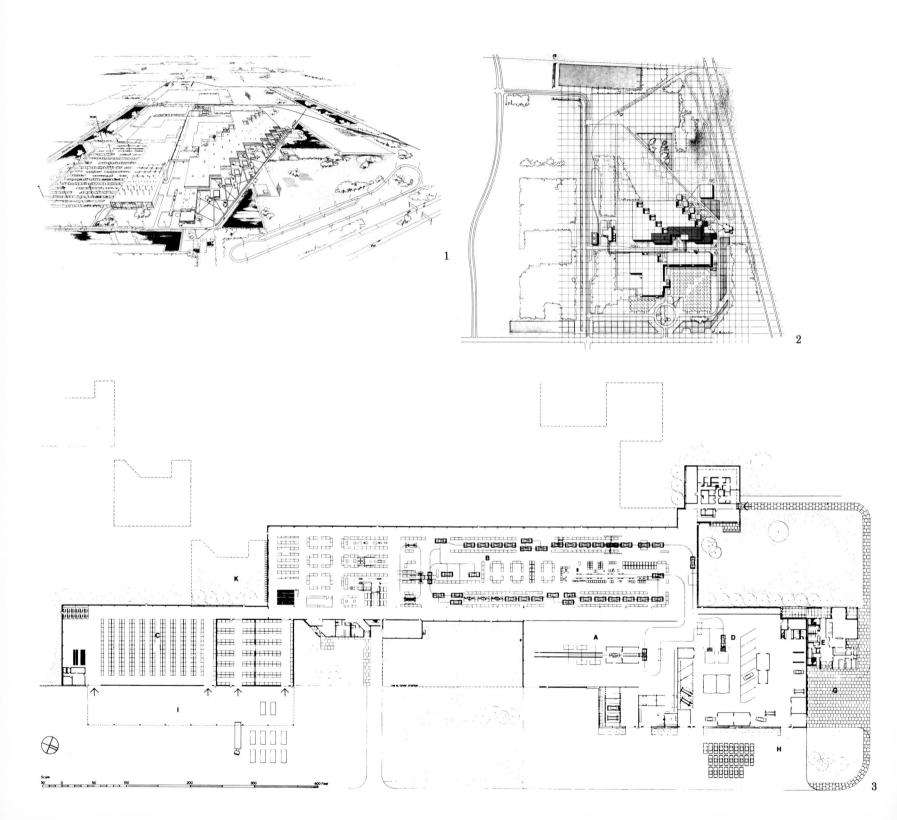

1

2

3

U.S. Car Manufacturing Division
Volvo of America Corporation
Chesapeake, Virginia 1976

Volvo's first automobile assembly plant in the United States was built on a 500 acre tract near Norfolk, Virginia. Construction proceeded simultaneously with design on a phased, fast-track schedule. The first phase, constructed in 1976, provides a capability of 20,000 cars per year in two shifts. It includes one of the several final assembly units, offices, the central mechanical plant, support facilities and worker amenities. Subsequent phases comprise a pre-delivery building, body assembly shop, paint shop and increased final assembly facilities. The master plan for the complex is scaled for an ultimate two shift capacity of 100,000 cars per year.

Because of a high water table, the low-lying flat site was developed with a series of large retaining lakes to control storm drainage. The various functions of the assembly process are separated and housed in individual but interrelated buildings to provide closed perimeters for independent incremental growth for each function. By having its own exterior walls, each unit can expand in several directions as needed. Material storage is kept inside or nearby each unit, reducing phasing and transport problems during the manufacturing process. Within the buildings, production flow is organized to free the exterior wall for the introduction of natural light, enhancing the working environment and providing constant visual contact for workers with the outdoors.

The concern for the individual working environment is also a strong determinant in the decision to separate the automated manufacturing sectors, such as metal stamping and painting, from the automobile assembly area staffed by workers. Each assembly area is designed as an individual "shop" containing a maximum of one hundred workers each. Within these shops, production allows the same group of workers to assemble each car as completely as possible, maintaining a continuous visual contact with the product of their labor to foster a sense of pride and identity.

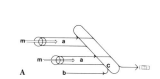

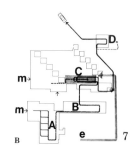

A) Production flow diagram

B) Site production flow diagram   7

9

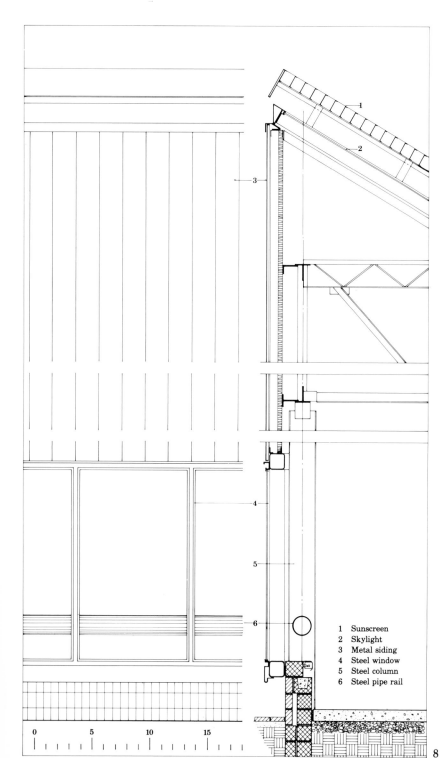

1 Sunscreen
2 Skylight
3 Metal siding
4 Steel window
5 Steel column
6 Steel pipe rail

0   5   10   15

8

10

A) Production flow diagram   7
B) Site production flow diagram
Section detail through west facade   8
Assembly phase window wall   9
Employee lockers   10
View from the west   11

11

1

1 Section and elevation through garden and courtyard
2 First floor plan
3 Site plan

CORPORATE HEADQUARTERS BUILDING
AB Volvo Holding Company
Gothenburg, Sweden 1984

The form of the Headquarters Building is determined by four major functional elements and their attendant services: the executive quarters, the corporate units, the visitors' areas, and the surrounding open spaces within the natural landscape. The building is approached by a roadway carefully laid within the fir forest that covers the headquarters' hilltop site. The road leads to an elongated entry circle flanking the main reception hall of the building. Reception, security and primary meeting facilities are housed in this hall and are linked by a glazed gallery along the inside of the central courtyard. Executive offices and conference rooms are on the ground floor and offices for visiting executives are on the upper level. Guest and staff dining facilities are on a lower level facing formal gardens.

The corporate portion of the building is by nature the largest sector; organized in "steps" along the western ridge of the site, the corporate units have offices which provide their occupants with views through the descending woods toward the sea. An emphasis on fine craftsmanship of natural materials is envisioned for the larger architectural elements of the building as well as in the more minute details of construction and interior finishes. This sense of craftsmanship functions as a metaphor for the value of human industry, a visible expression appropriate to the principles and style of the corporation.

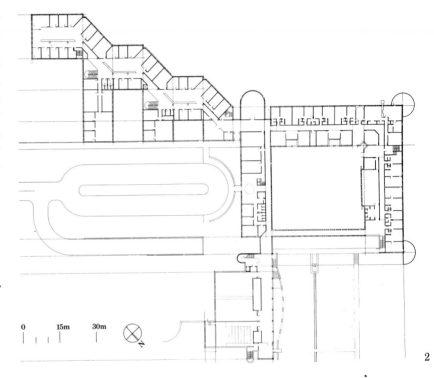

0   15m   30m

2

3

4

5

6

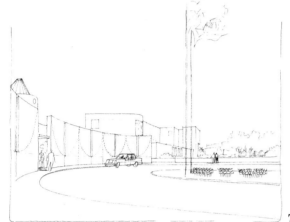

4 Southeast elevation
5 Northwest elevation
6 Aerial perspective of main entry
7 Sketch of entry
8 Sketch of garden terrace
9 Sketch of vestibule to auditorium
10 Model view

MAINTENANCE FACILITY, INDEPENDENCE PARK
National Park Service
Philadelphia, Pennsylvania 1981

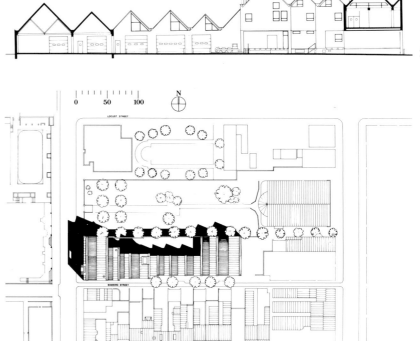

The Maintenance Facility is used by the National Park Service to house equipment needed for the care of the Independence Mall district in the center of Philadelphia. Included in the building are offices, material storage areas, and garages for trucks and other implements. The site is a narrow lot bordered by a venerable church and cemetery on one side and valuable historic townhouses of Philadelphia's Society Hill district on the other. In order to avoid the imposition of a barren, industrial scale building in this rich setting, a structure consisting of a sequence of small scale pitched roof bays was designed for the site. This sequence maintains the rhythm established by the facing townhouses, and provides the flanking cemetery with a quiet and intimate enclosure. Red brick masonry and metal roofs increase the building's sense of belonging to the traditional architecture characterizing this historic urban district. Glazed triangular openings in the walls allow ample natural light for illumination of interior storage and maintenance areas.

1 View from the northeast
2 Section looking south
3 Site plan
4 Detail of north elevation
5 Aerial view looking southwest

MANUFACTURING FACILITY MASTER PLAN
Knoll International
East Greenville, Pennsylvania 1984

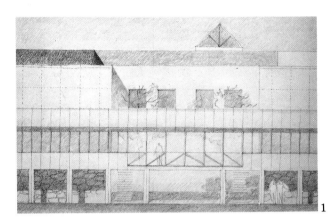

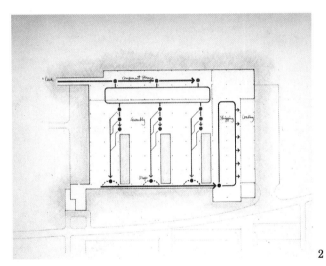

The recently completed master plan for Knoll International in East Greenville is organized according to a two-phase growth process. Phase 1 comprises an assembly-shipping facility linked to the existing building, support offices, a cafeteria and parking areas. Phase 2 expansion includes an additional assembly-shipping facility, an administrative building with showroom, sixteen double-occupancy guest quarters with dining and recreational facilities, additional parking for cars and fifty tractor trailers.

The master plan places the assembly-shipping facilities and guest quarters in a linear configuration parallel to adjacent railroad tracks and the administration building at the center of the site. The plan includes new internal roadways to minimize congestion with separate entrances and exits for trucks and cars. The landscaping enhances the linear organization of the master plan by locating a wooded area of deciduous trees at the center of the site, flanked by four linear rows of evergreens.

The design of the Phase 1 assembly-shipping facility organizes storage and assembly areas that accommodate the technology of robot cart storage and retrieval systems and also to enhance the environment of the individual worker. Separate high-bay component and shipping storage areas are at the rear periphery of the assembly area. A more human scale is achieved in the assembly area by lowering ceiling heights and by organizing assembly areas around three landscaped courts. These courtyards provide light, close visual proximity and access for workers to the outdoors throughout the workday.

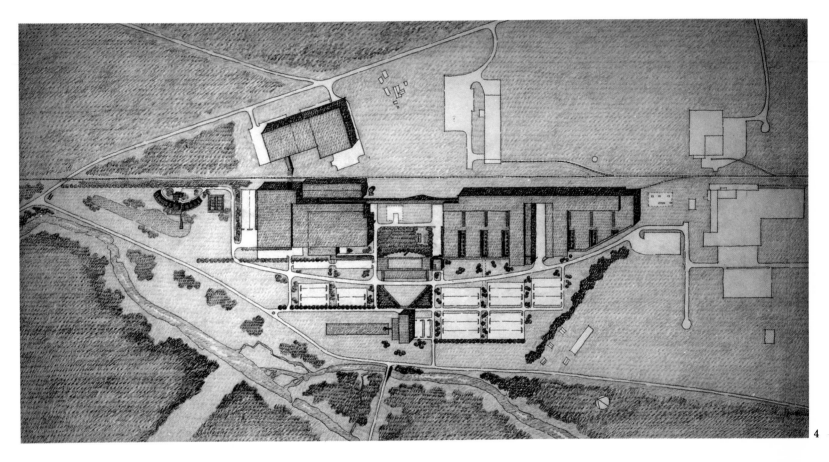

4

5

6

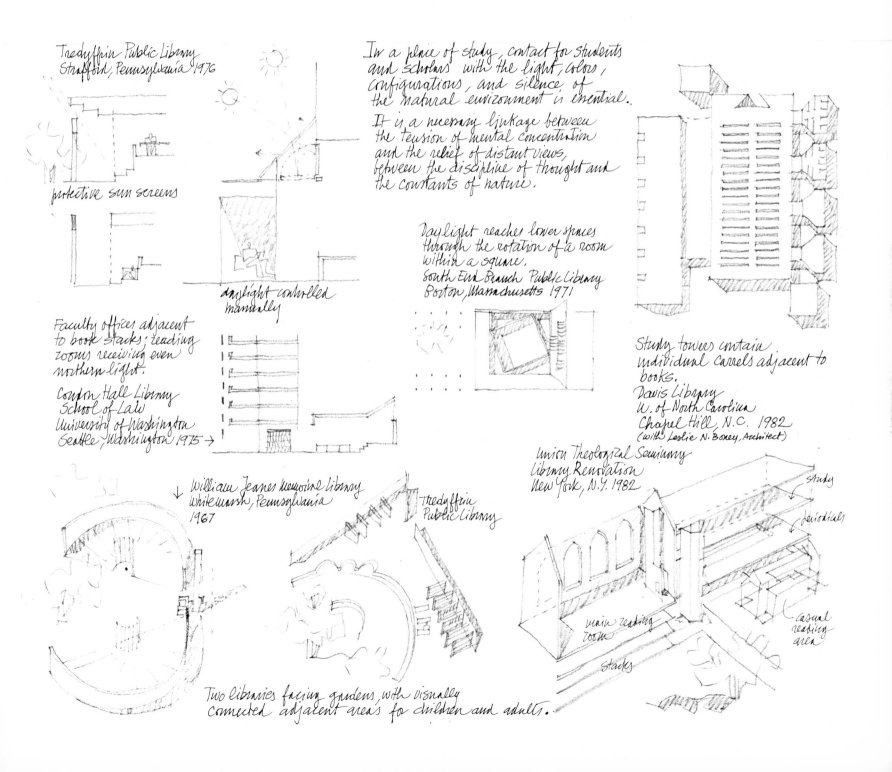

Tredyffrin Public Library
Strafford, Pennsylvania 1976

protective sun screens

daylight controlled manually

Faculty offices adjacent to book stacks; reading rooms receiving even northern light.
Condon Hall Library
School of Law
University of Washington
Seattle, Washington 1975 →

In a place of study, contact for students and scholars with the light, colors, configurations, and silence of the natural environment is essential.

It is a necessary linkage between the tension of mental concentration and the relief of distant views, between the discipline of thought and the constants of nature.

Daylight reaches lower spaces through the rotation of a room within a square.
South End Branch Public Library
Boston, Massachusetts 1971

Study towers contain individual carrels adjacent to books.
Davis Library
U. of North Carolina
Chapel Hill, N.C. 1982
(with Leslie N. Boney, Architect)

Union Theological Seminary
Library Renovation
New York, N.Y. 1982

study

periodicals

main reading room

casual reading area

stacks

↓ William Jeanes Memorial Library
Whitemarsh, Pennsylvania
1967

Tredyffrin
Public Library

Two libraries facing gardens, with visually connected adjacent areas for children and adults.

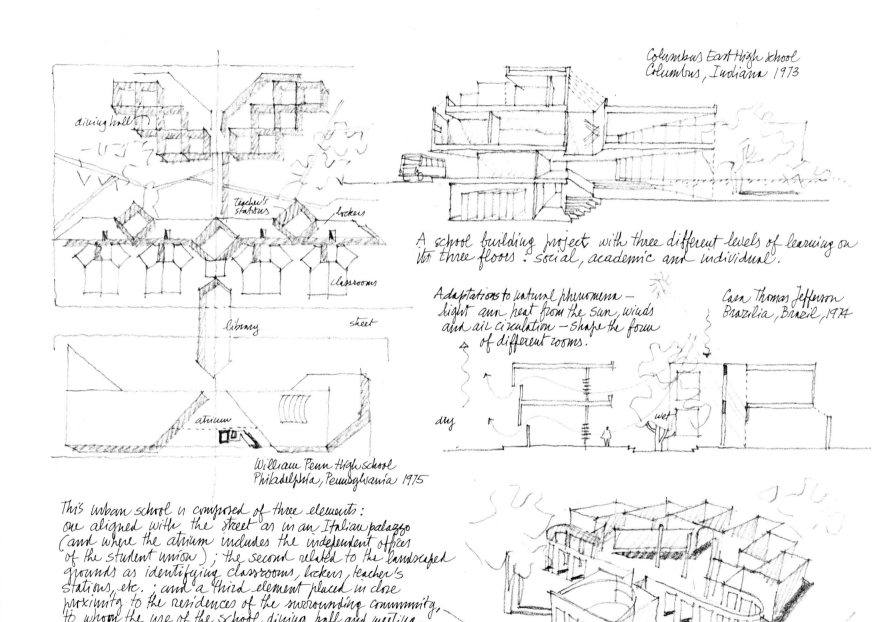

Columbus East High School
Columbus, Indiana 1973

A school building project with three different levels of learning on its three floors: social, academic and individual.

Adaptations to natural phenomena — light and heat from the sun, winds and air circulation — shape the form of different rooms.

Casa Thomas Jefferson
Brazilia, Brazil, 1974

dry

wet

dining hall

teacher's stations

lockers

classrooms

library

street

atrium

William Penn High school
Philadelphia, Pennsylvania 1975

This urban school is composed of three elements: one aligned with the street as in an Italian palazzo (and where the atrium includes the independent offices of the student union); the second related to the landscaped grounds as identifying classrooms, lockers, teacher's stations, etc.; and a third element placed in close proximity to the residences of the surrounding community, to whom the use of the school dining hall and meeting rooms are made freely available.

An elementary school whose form relates a narrative about the formality of social rapports: Aviano (Pordenone), Italy 1981

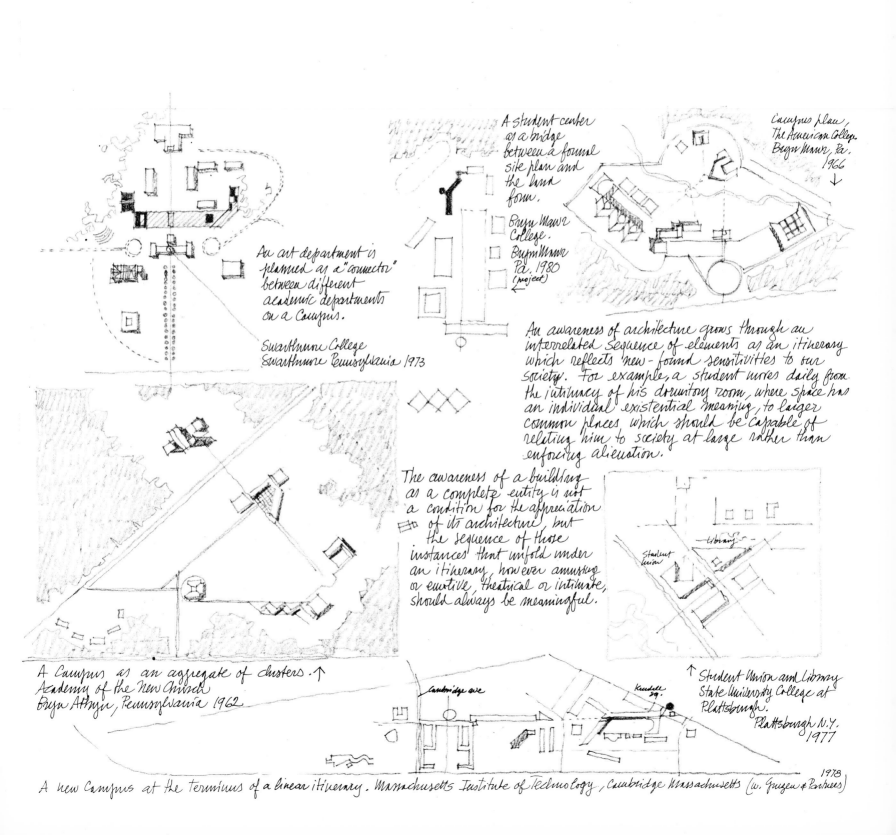

An art department is planned as a "connector" between different academic departments on a Campus.

Swarthmore College
Swarthmore Pennsylvania 1973

A student center as a bridge between a formal site plan and the land form.

Bryn Mawr College. Bryn Mawr Pa. 1980 (project)

Campus plan, The American College. Bryn Mawr, Pa. 1966

An awareness of architecture grows through an interrelated sequence of elements as an itinerary which reflects 'new-found' sensitivities to our society. For example, a student moves daily from the intimacy of his dormitory room, where space has an individual existential meaning, to larger common places which should be capable of relating him to society at large rather than enforcing alienation.

The awareness of a building as a complete entity is not a condition for the appreciation of its architecture, but the sequence of those instances that unfold under an itinerary, however amusing or emotive, theatrical or intimate, should always be meaningful.

Student Union   Library

A Campus as an aggregate of clusters. ↑
Academy of the New Church
Bryn Athyn, Pennsylvania 1962

Cambridge ave   Kendall sq.

↑ Student Union and Library
State University College at Plattsburgh.
Plattsburgh N.Y. 1977

1978
A new Campus at the terminus of a linear itinerary. Massachusetts Institute of Technology, Cambridge Massachusetts (w. Gruzen & Partners)

The administration building occupies a pivotal point on the campus of the Academy of the New Church, a Swedenborgian institution located on grassy fields in the Pennsylvania countryside. In symbolic terms the building is the center of a religious community which includes a church, a theological school and other facilities. The building is intentionally placed between the original school on the site and an augmented new campus. The three formal elements of the building's structure establish a directional relationship with the three important axes of the campus. The tripartite division of the building houses the Bishop's and Treasurer's offices, a board room and a rare books library, all flanking a central vestibule. The structure is entirely of bush-hammered poured-in-place reinforced concrete, with a lead coated copper roof.

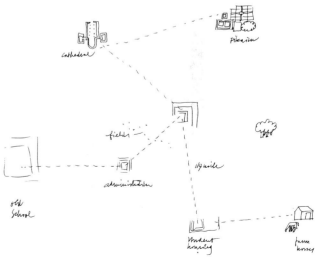

ADMINISTRATION BUILDING
Academy of the New Church
Bryn Athyn, Pennsylvania 1963

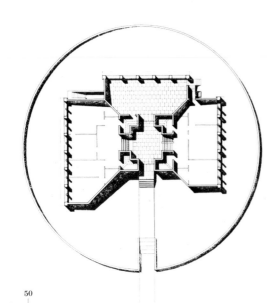

1 North elevation
2 Master plan sketch
3 First floor plan
4 Section perspective
5 North facade detail
6 Detail of facade

1 Aerial view of campus looking south
2 Site plan (1966)
3 Site sketch
4 Site plan: *1) Huebner Hall, 2) Myrick Pavilion, 3) Graduate Center,
  4) Service Building, 5) MDRT Foundation Hall*

From 1961 through 1966 a master plan for the development of the American College of Life Underwriters in Bryn Mawr was completed. At that time the campus consisted of a 32 acre site on rolling hills in the suburbs of Philadelphia. The center of the campus is a small valley defined by a stream with grand trees flanked by grassy fields. The master plan mandated the placement of college buildings along the crest of the hills overlooking the stream, thus enclosing the small valley, giving the college a sense of an internal space and a unified community within the perimeter established by the buildings. However, the college is both a closed, private entity and yet must remain open to the community at large, so must the buildings which form its perimeter be responsive to the surrounding community rather than forming a "fortress." As a result buildings primarily horizontal are placed on knolls and ridges at the periphery of the campus at wide intervals, so that they function as a defining yet accessible screen to the campus through which pedestrians can walk. Automobile circulation is restricted to the edges of the site.

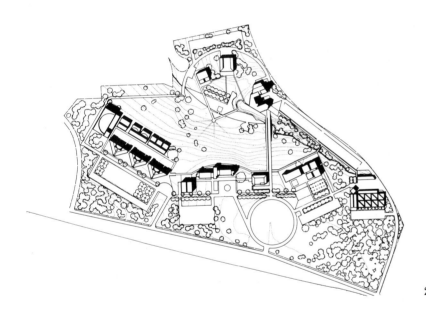

2

3

N

0   500

4

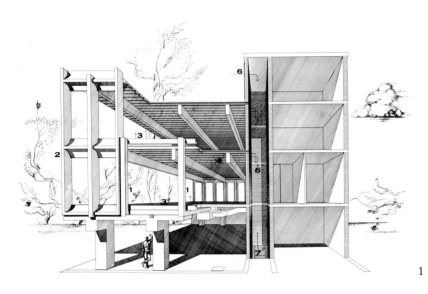

1

3

4

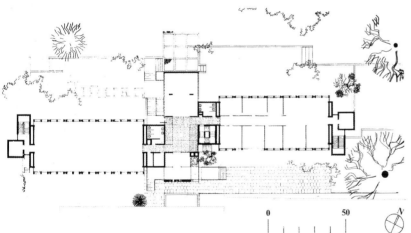

2

Section perspective: *1) riser duct to second floor, 2) precast concrete window unit, 3) horizontal perimeter air supply, 4) air return ports in cellular deck, 5) air return shaft, 6) fresh air intake, 7) air return trench* 1
First floor plan 2
Entry, southeast elevation 3
Facade detail 4
Main entry 5

5

HUEBNER HALL
MYRICK PAVILION
The American College
Bryn Mawr, Pennsylvania 1961, 1965

These two buildings were the first in a series of campus facilities constructed during a 20 year period for the American College. Huebner Hall was designed as the college's central administration building. Sited on a ridge overlooking a stream, the structure is composed of two separate wings joined by common facilities. Each wing contains two floors of column-free modular office space. The central core of the building functions as a place of entrance and reception, it houses archives, conference areas, service facilities and stairs. The ventilation system takes advantage of a hollow metal floor for the return air ducts, and air distribution is integrated into ducts placed within the structural wall window panels.

Myrick Pavilion is a previously existing carriage house which was renovated and expanded to house dining and conference facilities. The original stone exterior was preserved as the core of the building, around which an entry hall, dining rooms and kitchen services were added. The dining rooms also serve as seminar rooms.

2

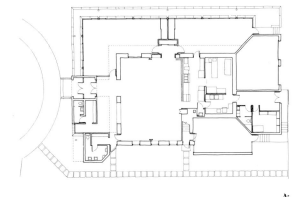

1

First floor plan 6
View from the west 7
Detail of main entry 8

3

MDRT FOUNDATION HALL
The American College
Bryn Mawr, Pennsylvania 1972

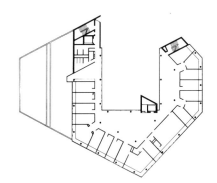

1

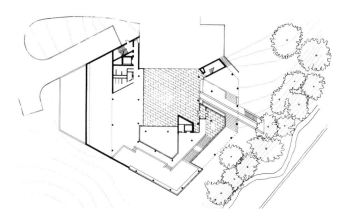

2

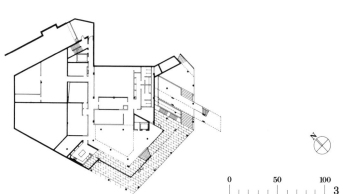

Foundation Hall is used as a research laboratory for the creation, sampling and evaluation of multimedia learning programs for continuing education in the insurance industry. The site is a promontory overlooking a stream and small lake with views to the east, south and west across a valley toward other existing college buildings.

The building is planned around an entrance court open on the north side to parking facilities and pedestrian walkways. The polygonal form of the facade responds to the topography of the site. Large spaces on the lower floors occupied by television and audio studios, which do not require daylight, form the solid base of the building. The major learning areas are on the ground floor and include a large divisible classroom with multimedia projection and T.V. capability, an audio workshop and small classroom. The first floor contains a library and audio/video carrels; these areas function together and are unified by a two-story central space. On the upper floors, the exterior wall encloses a series of executive offices and conference rooms oriented to views of the valley. The residual spaces formed by the inner walls of the court are used for secretarial pool spaces and circulation. The exterior finish of the building is frostproof ceramic facing tile placed over a poured-in-place reinforced concrete structural frame.

```
0        50       100
|ıııııı|ııııı|  3
```

Third and fourth floor plans: *conference, study rooms* 1
First floor: *library, visitor orientation* 2
Ground floor: *group areas, workshop, television studio* 3
View from the west 4
View from the north 5

4

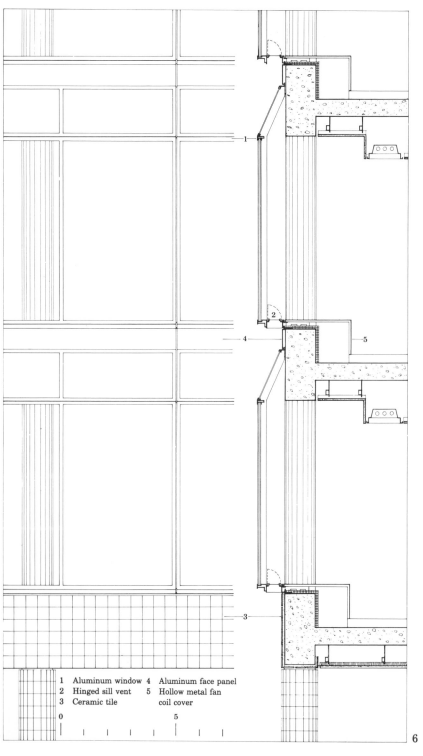

1. Aluminum window   4. Aluminum face panel
2. Hinged sill vent   5. Hollow metal fan
3. Ceramic tile   coil cover

0   5

6

7

8

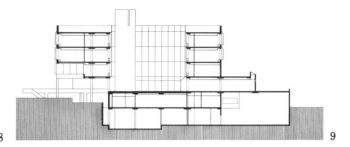

9

10

11

12

1   View from the north
2   View from the south
3   View of north courtyard
4   Second floor plan: *classroom, residence rooms*
5   First floor plan: *lounge, television center, lecture hall, lobby, residence rooms*
6   Lower floor plan: *dining, kitchen, services*
7   Site study model

GRADUATE CENTER
The American College
Bryn Mawr, Pennsylvania 1981

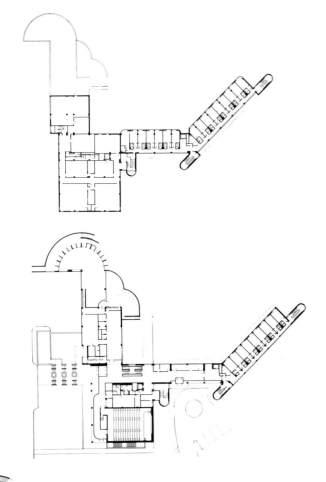

The Graduate Center is a single building within which three major functions are contained: conference and academic facilities, classrooms, offices and an auditorium; a residential wing for students; and a dining hall serving the entire American College campus. The site is at the crest of a small rolling valley. The center is a horizontal structure which visually closes the valley but imposes only a modest massing on the hill's crest. The residential wing is above ground on pylons, which allows pedestrians to walk uninterrupted while establishing a sense of visual termination for the northeast corner of the campus.

The three functions of the building are expressed by three separate wings joined by lobbies and lounge areas: an academic building on the south, dining wing on the north, and dormitory wing on the east. This elongated plan creates a variety of spaces, experiences and views for the visitor or resident and provides busy or quiet places, sunlit or shaded.

4

5

7

0   50   100   150

6

124

8 Sketch of dining pavilions
9 Lecture hall
10 Detail of north facade
11 Central staircase
12 View of residence rooms from the north
13 Detail of dining pavilion

8

9

10

11

12

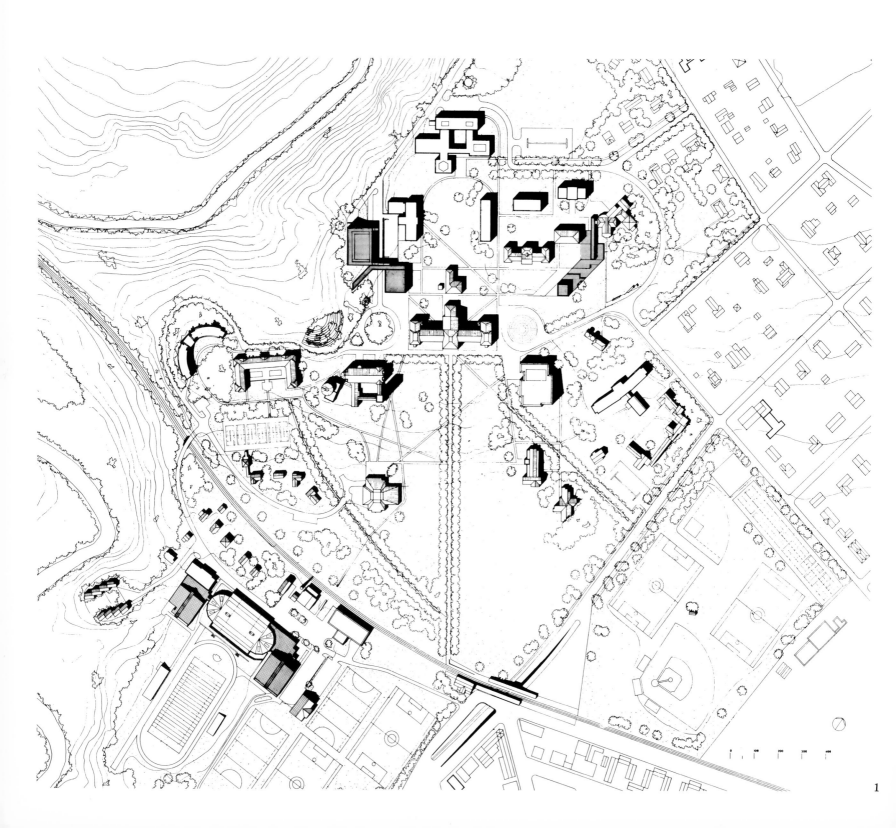

CAMPUS PLAN UPDATING
EUGENE M. AND THERESA LANG
MUSIC BUILDING
Swarthmore College
Swarthmore, Pennsylvania 1970-1978, 1973

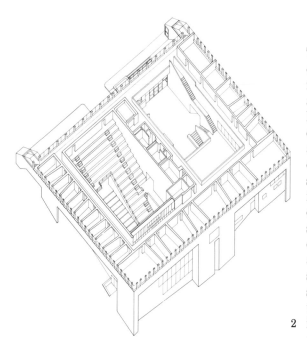

The music building completed in 1974 is part of a master plan developed by the firm in 1970 for the accommodation of the arts at Swarthmore. The plan positions buildings for the study of music, performing arts and the visual arts in a central band of space between the Main Building, Parrish Hall and the various academic buildings of the campus. This location demonstrates a new regard at Swarthmore for art as a proper part of life, and the music building was the first to be constructed. The heavily wooded site chosen for the music building slopes steeply away from the campus. The 450-seat concert hall is inserted into the hillside so that its mass does not intrude on the rest of the campus. The hall is divided into two parts each with a different slope, bringing the traditional balcony in direct contact with the orchestra level. This provides access to the auditorium from the practice and classroom levels on the top floor, increasing accessibility to the students, and in addition making the large space more comfortable for small groups when the room is not filled. The end wall of the auditorium is glazed to allow views into the woods beyond. The construction is highly sophisticated acoustically so that all areas may be used at once without interference. The acoustics of the concert hall can be altered to modify its brightness, and special treatments have been developed for flute, piano and cello practice rooms. Exposed gray concrete was chosen for its dense acoustic mass; this color also relates to the gray stone of the surrounding buildings.

Campus plan, shaded buildings indicate proposed 1
buildings
Axonometric of music building 2
Conceptual sketch 3
Aerial view looking west 4

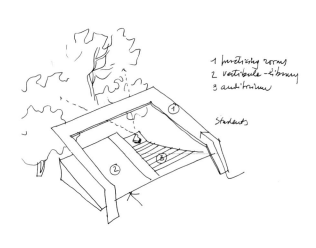

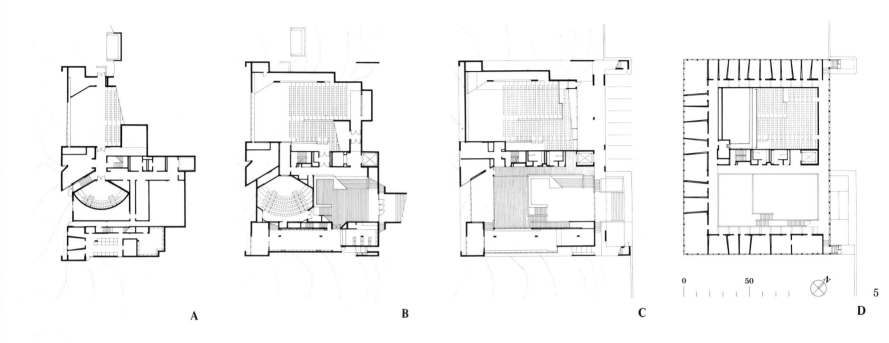

A   B   C   D

0   50   5

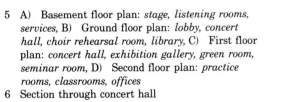

5 A) Basement floor plan: *stage, listening rooms,*
   services, B) Ground floor plan: *lobby, concert*
   hall, choir rehearsal room, library, C) First floor
   plan: *concert hall, exhibition gallery, green room,*
   seminar room, D) Second floor plan: *practice*
   rooms, classrooms, offices
6 Section through concert hall

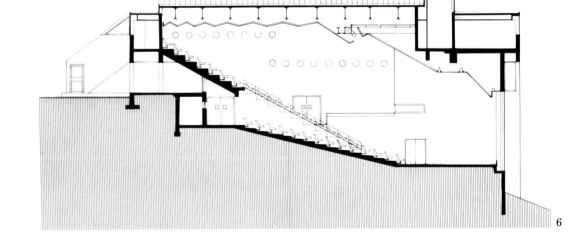

6

7   View from the south
8   Practice room corridor
9   Detail of southwest facade

10 Concert hall stage
11 Entrance lobby and exhibition gallery
12 Concert hall
13 Lobby staircase and library entry
14 Detail of northeast facade

15 Concert hall
16 Library
17-20 Concert hall

PHYSICAL ACTIVITIES BUILDING
Swarthmore College
Swarthmore, Pennsylvania 1979

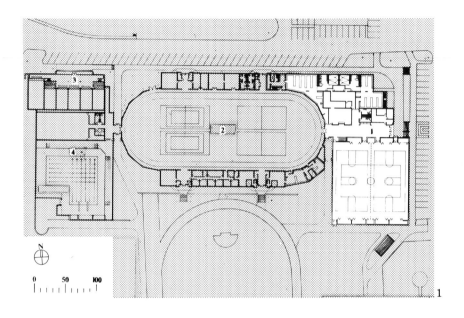

Plan of sports complex: 1
1) physical activities building
with flexible gym, 2) existing
arena, 3) existing squash courts,
4) proposed pool
View from the south 2

1   Acrylic skylight
2   Built-up roof
3   Stucco
4   3-Dimensional pipe truss
5   Nylon netting
6   Heat and ventilation unit

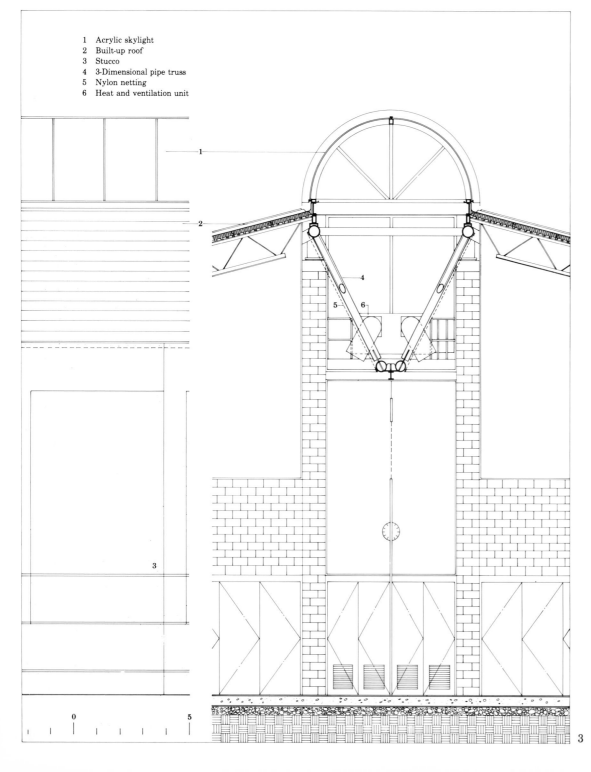

0   5

3

4

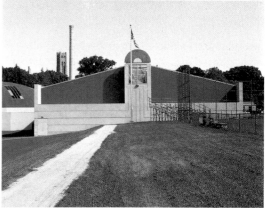

5

3   Section detail through skylight
4   Gymnasium with central partition closed
5   North elevation
6   South elevation
7   Detail of south facade

This Physical Activities Building was designed to provide indoor facilities for newly combined men's and women's physical education departments at the college. Adjacent to the existing Lamb-Miller Field House and practice fields the new structure provides auxiliary practice space and allows maximum sharing of facilities such as showers, locker rooms, laundry, equipment storage and training rooms.

The major element of the building is a "flexible gymnasium," so-called because the 120 feet square, column-free space functions primarily as a practice area which can be divided to accommodate various simultaneous activities. In addition, the existing perimeter spaces which flank the Lamb-Miller arena floor were renovated to house necessary offices, classrooms and visiting team locker rooms.

The external form of the building is defined by structural piers which support a roof truss and the multicolored end panel of the vaulted skylight. Extending the full length of the axis of the gymnasium, the skylight supplies natural illumination to the interior of the practice spaces.

Materials were chosen to be in harmony with existing campus buildings: concrete masonry walls covered with unpainted stucco, red brick band courses and red metal siding on the end walls, which relates to the painted wood siding of a neighboring red barn. Detailing was kept simple and direct in accord with adjacent structures, reflecting the Quaker tradition of the college.

6

7

STUDENT UNION
STATE UNIVERSITY COLLEGE
AT PLATTSBURGH
New York State University Construction Fund
Plattsburgh, New York 1974

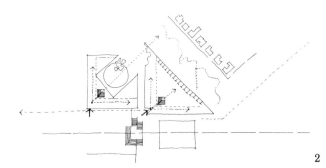

2

The Student Union forms part of an enclosure for a two-level paved plaza at the academic center of this campus for 5,000 students. The union contains a bookstore, cafeterias for 400 students, a large banquet room and a variety of lounges, meeting rooms and workshops.

The variety of functions of the student union is expressed in a series of diverse, individualized spatial experiences and vistas. The spaces are organized around open, 50-foot wide corridors wrapping around the courtyard, which acts as a continual focus for orientation. Fully glazed walls permit the cafeterias on both sides of the court to be closely related to the diagonal green space beyond their walls. Because of a high water table, mechanical equipment is above ground level in the building which expands the volume of the student union. This improves the visual relationship of the union to the mass of surrounding buildings by emphasizing its presence, which symbolically centers upon the importance of the welfare of the students.

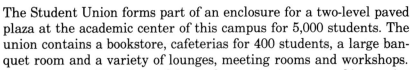

3

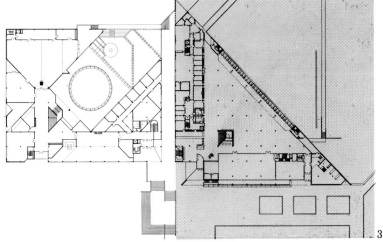

0   100

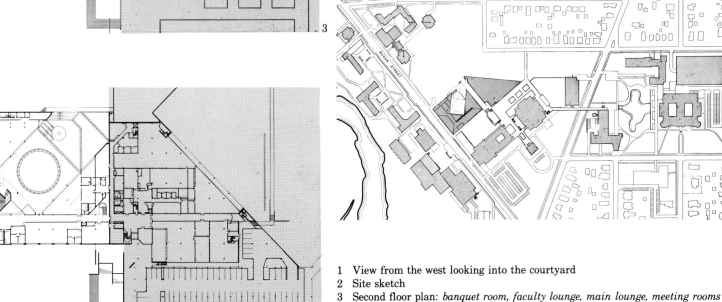

5

1 View from the west looking into the courtyard
2 Site sketch
3 Second floor plan: *banquet room, faculty lounge, main lounge, meeting rooms*
4 First floor plan: *cafeteria, kitchen, bookstore, snack bar*
4 5 Campus plan

6

7

8

9

10

11

12

BENJAMIN F. FEINBERG LIBRARY
STATE UNIVERSITY COLLEGE
AT PLATTSBURGH
New York State University Construction Fund
Plattsburgh, New York 1977

At the main exterior stair which connects the two levels of the paved plaza forming the center of the Plattsburgh campus, the Library and the Student Union create a gateway between the teaching and administrative areas and the social and residential areas beyond. The flat eight acre site for the two buildings is at an intersection of two city grid systems. Both structures derive their triangular forms from the interrelation of these grids. The diagonally cut courtyard of the student union and the western face of the library reconcile the town's secondary axis with the orthogonal grid of the campus plan. These facades are oriented toward a series of stepped greens which contrast in character with the paved plazas at the front of the buildings.

The library is a flexible open stack facility containing 250,000 volumes and extensive non-book areas. The reader/stack area is the major space of the building, and is oriented with views to the west. Light filters into this space through windows flanking two layers of private carrels. The large formal reading rooms of the special collections area face the campus plaza, where their fully glazed facades allow views toward the courtyard's activity to enliven the library's quiet solitude.

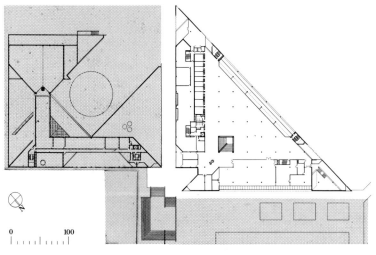

0   100

2

1 Special collections study area
2 Third floor plan: *stack and reading area, special collections, seminar rooms*
3 West elevation
4 Upper plaza main entries for student union and library
1 5 Detail of northeast facade

3

4

5

6

7

8

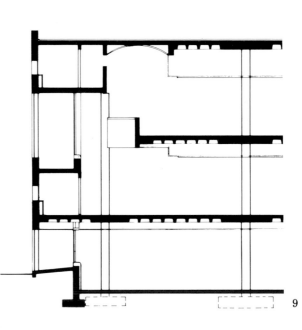

9

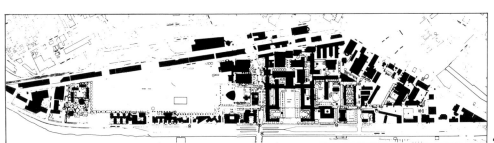

Aerial view 1
Existing campus site coverage plan 2
Baldwin rendered plan 3

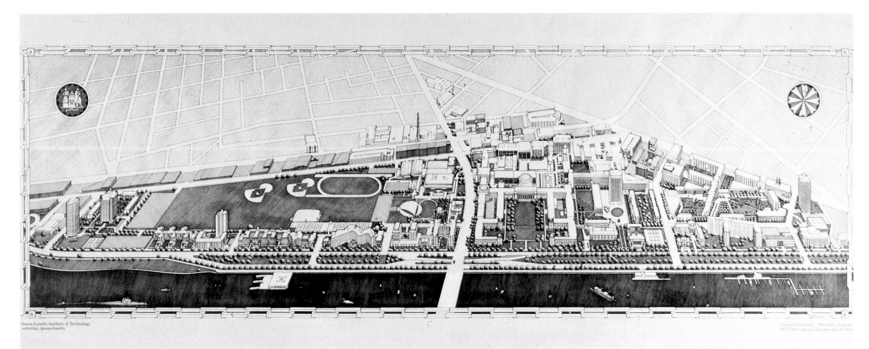

EAST CAMPUS DEVELOPMENT PLAN
Massachusetts Institute of Technology
Cambridge, Massachusetts 1978
With Gruzen & Partners

The new East Campus is a largely undeveloped, 14 acre site, designed to provide a new synthesis of the academic, environmental and community objectives of the school. The master plan addresses questions of land use, development capabilities, circulation, parking, landscaping and prototypical building design. At the time of development of the plan, the East Campus area was characterized by the presence of light industry and other older buildings renovated for administrative and staff functions of MIT. The spatial intent of the plan is to formulate development of a linear extension of the existing campus. Open to Kendall Square at one corner, the elongated quadrangle completes an on campus itinerary beginning at Massachusetts Avenue and continuing on an axis parallel to the Charles River. The quadrangle is a central open space flanked by academic buildings, each with a portico facing the landscaped area. A founding principle for the design is continuation of the strong MIT campus tradition of interior continuity via the main "street" or internal corridor. This characteristic internal passage was later carried into the East Campus in the form of a skylit arcade which connects the Health Services and Health Sciences buildings, completed in 1981, and provides linkages for future East Campus structures. The linkage and juxtaposition between this internal campus circulation corridor and the Kendall Square frontage on the East Campus is important, as it provides MIT with a crucial connection to a commercial district of the city.

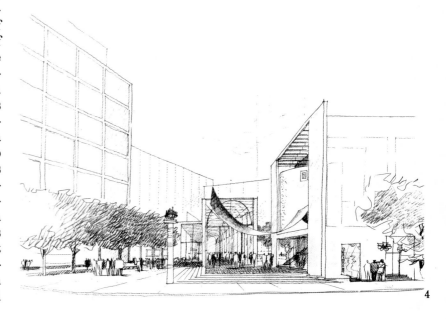

4

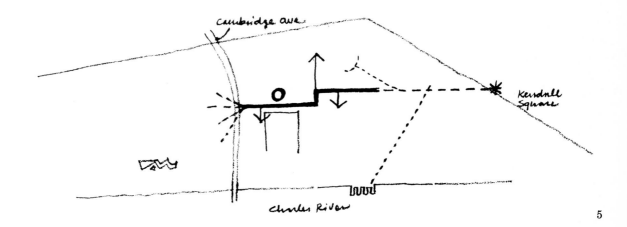

5

4 East campus gateway
5 Conceptual site diagram

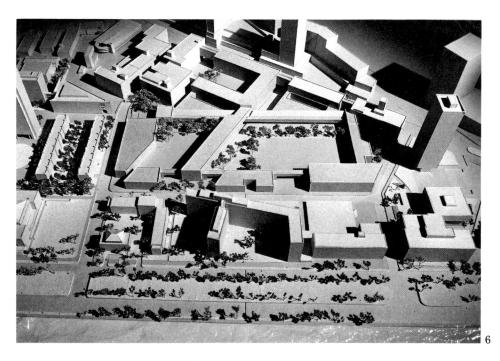

6

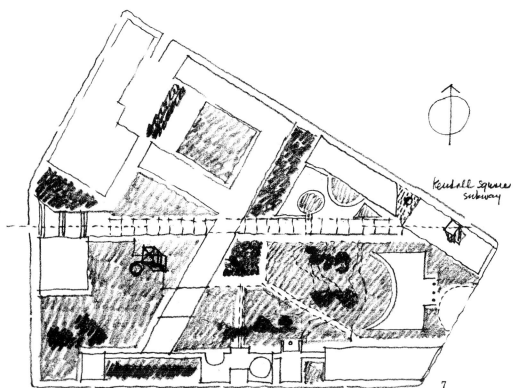

Kendall square
subway

7

6 Site model
7 Sketch plan

8

health services   subway   east campus   9

8 Galleria
9 Subway entry from the central court
10 10 Sculpture court

HEALTH SERVICES BUILDING
COLLEGE OF HEALTH SCIENCES, TECHNOLOGY AND MANAGEMENT BUILDING
Massachusetts Institute of Technology
Cambridge, Massachusetts 1981
With Gruzen & Partners

The Health Sciences/Health Services complex on MIT's East Campus is composed of two buildings united by a common atrium. The design of the complex was initiated with two separate programs and exist in a mutually supportive medical and scientific relationship. The Health Sciences, Technology and Management Building forms the northern wing extending from the central five-story atrium linking the two buildings. Laboratories are on five floors above grade, with the ground floor reserved for more public activities such as classrooms, lecture halls and a large reading room. The dark red brick on the exterior of the building and granite edged teak windows were selected as a warm contrast to the concrete and limestone vocabulary prevalent on the main campus. The precast concrete arcade provides visual continuity with the predominant grey coloration of most campus buildings. The Health Services Building forms the southern wing of the complex and houses the MIT Medical Service and Infirmary, which provides medical care for 40,000 students, faculty, staff and family members, functioning on a "walk-in" basis and as a subscription health maintenance organization. The plan of the Health Services wing functions as an "ocean liner" of small offices and examination rooms contiguous to a series of waiting rooms. In spite of the complexity of this configuration, a short and easily intelligible route is followed by the patient between the building entrance and the doctor's office.

1

2

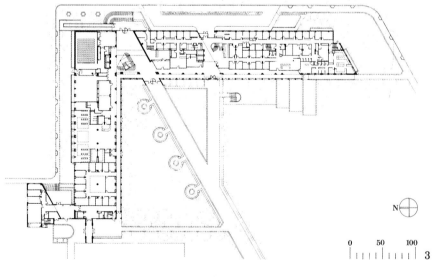

N

0   50   100

3

View from the west 1
Aerial view from the east 2
First level plan: *atrium, lecture hall, labs,* 3
offices, conference, library
Laboratory 4
Lecture hall 5
Atrium ceiling 6
Atrium staircase 7

Arcade 8, 9
Section detail through arcade 10
View from the west 11

8

9

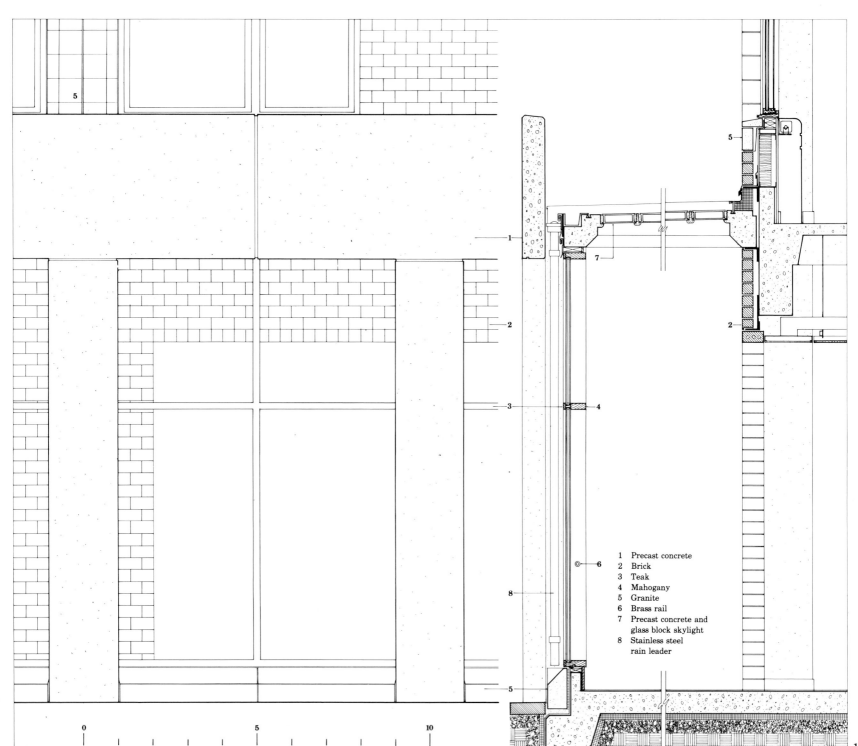

1 Precast concrete
2 Brick
3 Teak
4 Mahogany
5 Granite
6 Brass rail
7 Precast concrete and
  glass block skylight
8 Stainless steel
  rain leader

0   5   10

10

SHERMAN FAIRCHILD CENTER FOR THE LIFE SCIENCES
Columbia University
New York, New York 1977

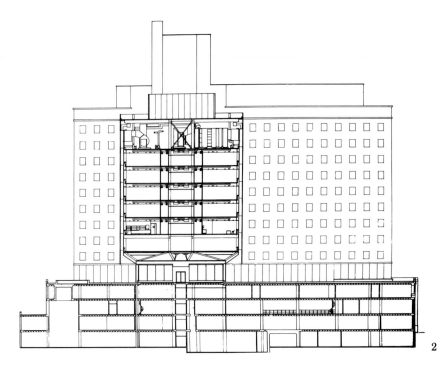

The Fairchild Center houses the Department of Biology in an environment of high quality, and includes laboratory facilities and support spaces, conference rooms and administrative offices. The site was limited and complex: the new building was to be set atop an existing podium structure containing a lounge and five floors of service facilities tightly surrounded by three academic buildings of disparate architectural styles and character. The design developed for the building organizes the space around a definition of the department's two programmatic elements: a nine story unit for laboratories and service spaces, and a seven story unit that contains communal and administrative areas. Laboratory work areas are placed at the perimeter of the building, service and circulation areas are located at the center. Supply air is completely exhausted from the building to eliminate the spread of contaminants, but a heat recovery system captures the heat from exhaust air. Shafts for the exhaust ducts are on the exterior of the building, and also provide the structure for a double layer exterior wall system composed of an inner aluminum and glass curtain wall, and an outer layer of precast concrete panels faced with warm red tile. This "outer skin" shades the inner curtain wall on the east, south and west elevations and complements the existing neo-Georgian buildings.

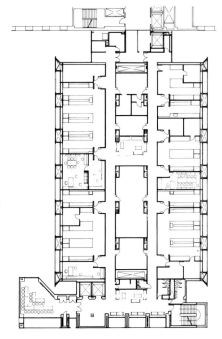

Southwest elevation 1
Section looking northeast 2
Site plan 3
Model view 4
Typical floor plan 5

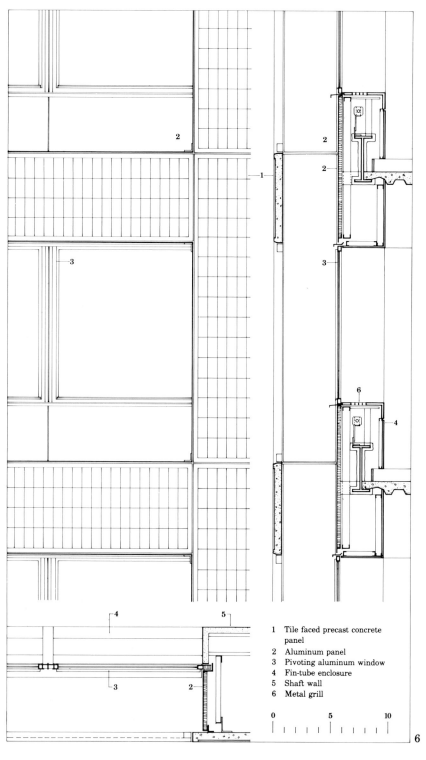

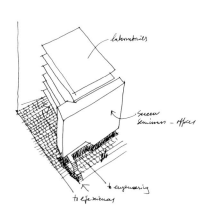

1   Tile faced precast concrete
    panel
2   Aluminum panel
3   Pivoting aluminum window
4   Fin-tube enclosure
5   Shaft wall
6   Metal grill

0   5   10

6

7

8

9

10

12

13

11

14

CONDON HALL, SCHOOL OF LAW
University of Washington
Seattle, Washington 1975

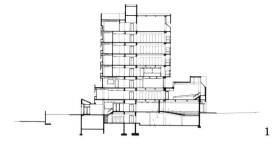

1

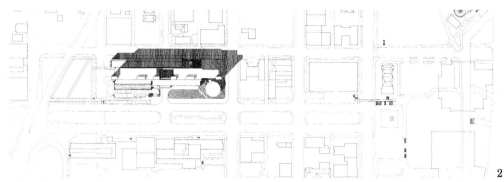

2

N

0   50

3

4

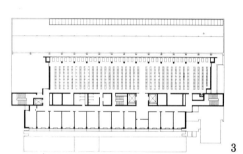

5

6

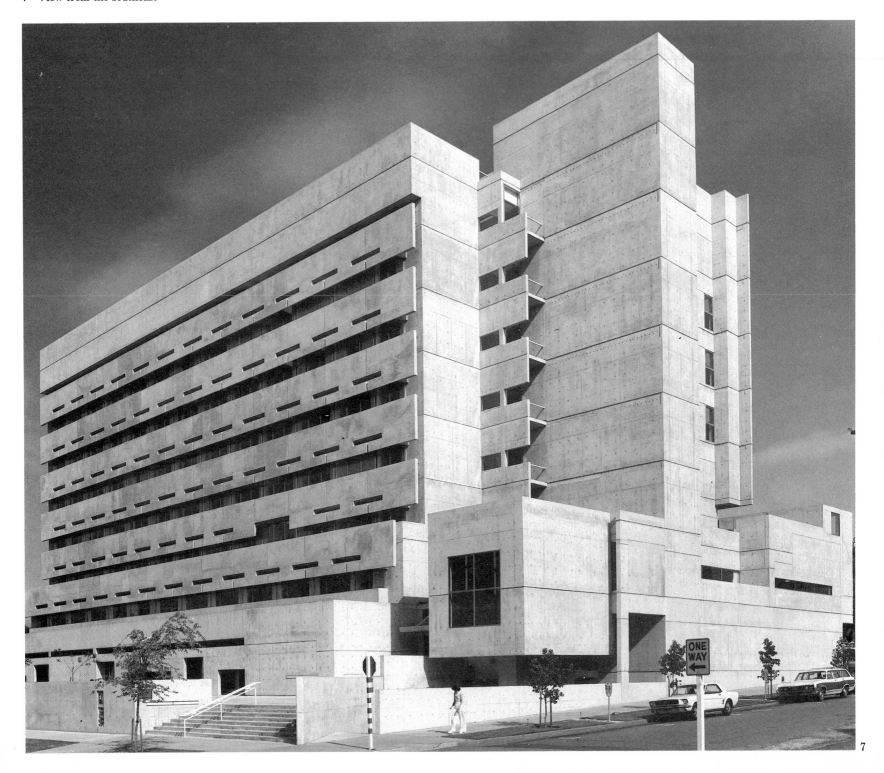

7

The design for the School of Law consists of a linear building placed on a long, narrow site. Construction was planned in two phases: the first phase structure accommodates 500 students and a library of 250,000 volumes; the second phase facilities for 50 postgraduate students will be added and the library capacity doubled.

In the Phase 1 structure, classrooms, seminar rooms, the moot court, student facilities, lockers and lounges are on the ground floor of the building to allow direct access from the outside to these highly used areas. The second floor contains the reading room and the technical services of the law library; this location above the street level provides isolation from noise. Clerestories and skylights provide diffused natural light throughout the reading room. Administrative offices, the faculty lounge and a library occupy the third floor. All offices face south and library stacks are adjacent to the northern elevation; a bank of service facilities forming a linear core for the building separates office areas from the stacks. These three functions are clearly expressed on the ends of the building where the reinforced concrete construction, exposed as cast, is revealed. Precast cladding is used above the third floor on the north facade where reading carrels are placed and precast units on the south protect offices from low solar angles during the winter months.

8

8 First floor corridor
9 Library gallery
10 Main entry from staircase tower
11 Library looking west

9

10

TREDYFFRIN PUBLIC LIBRARY
Tredyffrin Township
Strafford, Pennsylvania 1976

This community library with a capacity for 60,000 volumes is at the uppermost point of Strafford Park in the rolling Philadelphia suburbs. The organization of the building places book storage and workspaces toward the street and reading spaces toward the park. Meeting and conference rooms, the staff lounge and mechanical spaces are on the lower level. The building is inserted into the hillside so that both floors have direct access into the park. The solid entrance elevation, pierced only by the entryway and skylights, maintains the low profile of its residential neighbors and preserves views of the park's mature trees from the street. Reading rooms for children and adults are placed along a curved glass wall facing the park. The wood ceilings of the reading rooms slope up to clerestory windows admitting a balanced natural light. Intimate built-in seats are located along the edge of the glass wall, as is the large stair in the children's area utilized for "story time." Paralleling the curved glass wall is a freestanding concrete wall which provides both a backdrop for terrace activities and year-round solar control.

1

Site plan 1
First floor plan 2
View from the south 3

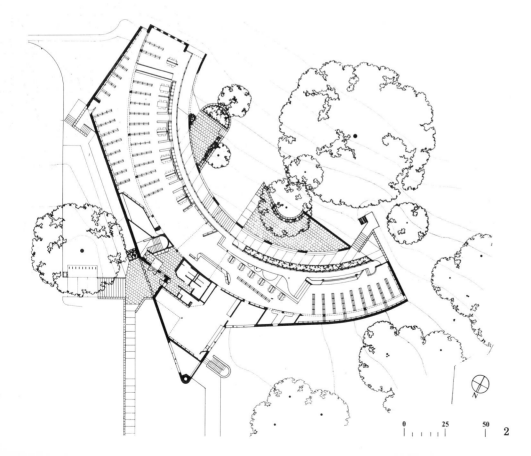

0   25   50   2

View from the north 4
Main entry 5
Screen wall 6
Detail of screen wall looking northeast 7

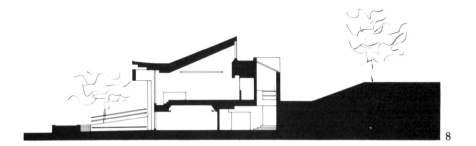

8

9

10

11

12　12　Reading alcoves

13

13 View from the south
14 General reading area

14

SOUTH END BRANCH PUBLIC LIBRARY
City of Boston
Boston, Massachusetts 1971

This library is in the center of a low income, mixed neighborhood in an area undergoing intense reconstruction, both private and governmental. Its surroundings are an eloquent reminder of nineteenth century Boston: three story brick buildings, semicircular bay windows, uniform cornice heights and mansard roofs. The way of life of the neighborhood's new population generates a gregarious and active use of the public place. The siting of the library, placed at the short end of the block and occupying less than half of the lot, leaves a generous green court and walkway, furnished with benches for the public and shaded by a wood trellis.

The building consists of two floors, with two reading rooms on the ground floor and community areas on the second floor. A basement level was not possible because of a high water table. The adult reading room occupies the center of the building and is surrounded by a band of spaces which filter light into it. The charge counter and office have a view of the street and protect the southern exposure of the reading room, several reading alcoves facing the grass court shield the west exposure. The room receives light from a clerestory window which surrounds the base of the community rooms upstairs and is modulated by a system of hand operated panels allowing for localized sun control. The dual stairs which lead to community rooms form an archway on the ground floor between the adult reading room and the children's library, providing a functional sense of separation between the two spaces without the presence of an actual physical barrier.

1 Detail of southeast elevation
2 Detail of southwest elevation
3 Main entry
4 First floor plan

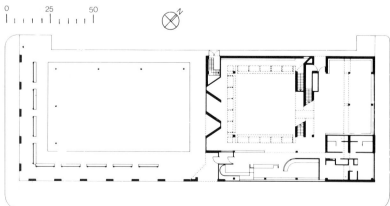

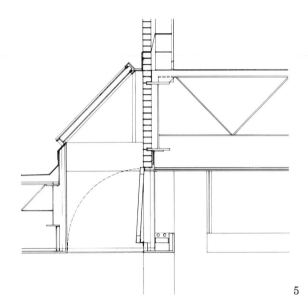

Skylight detail 5
Reading room ceiling 6
Reading room 7

LIBRARY RENOVATION
BOOKSTORE AND LOUNGE
Union Theological Seminary
New York, New York 1980, 1982

The Library at Union Theological Seminary functions as the heart of that institution. It provides a community of scholars with a collection of international importance consisting of a general collection of over 500,000 volumes and an extensive rare book collection. Accommodated in a Gothic Revival building erected in 1908, the library is in the seminary's academic quadrangle on Manhattan's Upper West Side. A new bookstore and a commons or lounge area was completed in advance of the main renovation project to create a new focal point for social interaction previously lacking at the seminary. The reorganization of the library's six floors of space is based upon recognition that the expanding collection is being utilized by an increasingly more diverse community. Renovation began at street level with a prominent new entryway, followed by a new two-story space in which prospective readers are oriented to the whole of the library. Numerous reading spaces have been developed throughout the upper floors of the building, including individual study rooms where scholars work in total isolation, a large reference reading room which seats 60 readers and a terrace reading room with glazed walls for views to the outdoors. Security, fire safety, access for handicapped readers and climate control for book preservation are substantially improved in the renovated building. Interior finishes and furnishings are designed to coexist with the Gothic Revival style of the building without mimicking its forms.

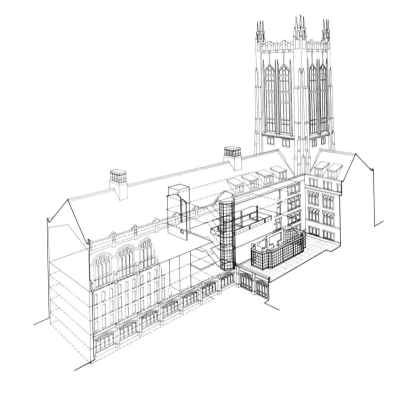

1

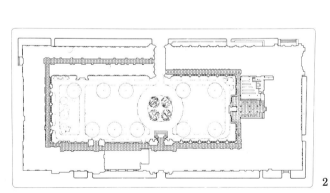

2

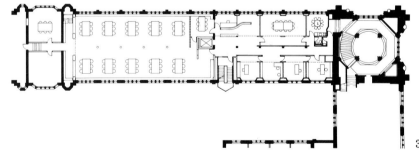

3

Axonometric showing new construction 1
Site plan with new bookstore and lounge 2
Third floor plan: *main reading room, reference, rare* 3
books, reading, offices
First floor plan: *entry, bibliography, terrace reading* 4
room, stacks

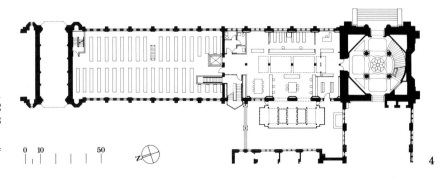

0 10   50

4

5

6

7

5 Main reading room
6 Bookstore
7 New stairway and terrace reading room from the
 courtyard

1

GEOLOGY LIBRARY
Princeton University
Princeton, New Jersey 1980

1 View from the southeast
2 Site plan
3 Partial campus plan
4 Main floor plan: *A) geology department, B) geology library, C) biology department*

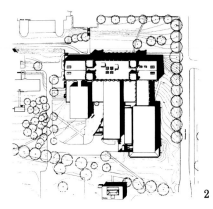

2

This library project consisted of renovation and construction of an addition to Guyot Hall, which houses the Departments of Biology and Geology and the Museum of Natural History. A major requirement of the new library was the unification of the disparate elements of the building, since four other additions had already been made to the Hall, all of which were of diverse materials and colors. At a time when the design was initiated, the southern approach to the building was dominated by two laboratory additions surrounded by a congested area of parking and loading docks. The final design solution placed the new linear two level library addition between the existing laboratories. This solution not only preserved the handsome original north elevation, but also allowed a landscaped pedestrian court and separate loading dock on the south, thus redefining the approach to the building and eliminating the previous confusion of function between access and service.

The library is entered through the Museum of Natural History, giving a new vitality and life to the area surrounding the display exhibits. The renovation of the main floor museum space incorporated part of the library into the south side of the Hall, utilizing an existing mezzanine to define the new two level spaces of the library addition. A circulation spine on the west side of the new wing provided access to a variety of spaces of differing functions and forms—bookstacks, a map room and study carrels. Reading areas for small groups are along the western wall, allowing exterior views through large windows into the landscaped court.

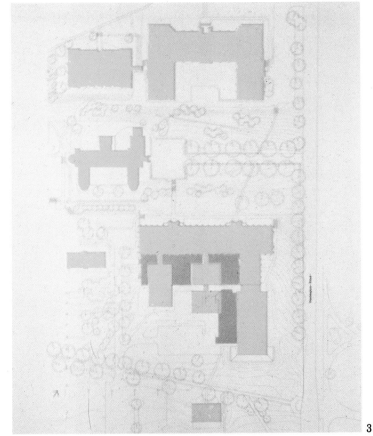

3

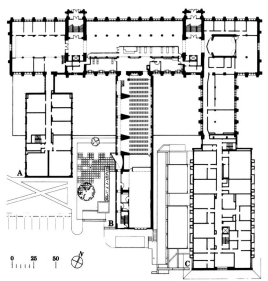

0 25 50

4

5

6

7

8

9

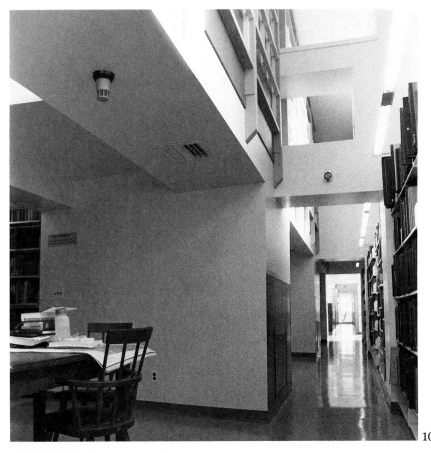

10

11

12 Mezzanine reading area
13 View from the south
14 Map room
15 Southeast elevation

University of Pennsylvania
Philadelphia, Pennsylvania 1984

B ⊥ A   2

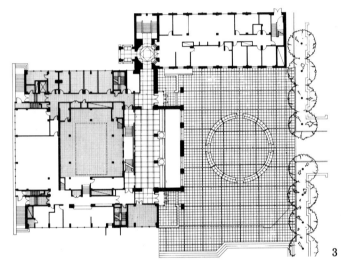

3

N⊕

0   50

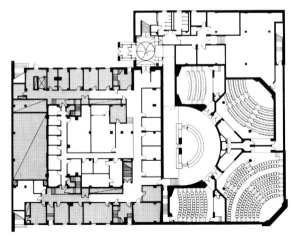

4

1   Courtyard sketch looking northeast
2   Section: *A) new construction, B) existing building with unrenovated areas shaded*
3   First floor plan
4   Basement floor plan
5   Site model

This expansion project combines a building addition, selected renovations of the existing Annenberg School building and functional reorganization to create a new unified facility. The expanded and renovated structure is intended not only to provide needed space but also to focus pedestrian circulation, to create a strong sense of visual identity for the school and to improve the adjacent plaza as a vital part of the Annenberg complex.

The building addition is a single structure comprised of three major elements: a three story office and service wing, an atrium extension to the existing lobby and a classroom wing placed under the Annenberg Plaza. The office wing is along the east side of the plaza to complete the physical definition of its space. As a result, the plaza gains a strong identity as a courtyard and it becomes an "outdoor room" with the school building facades as walls. The rectangular shape of the office wing accommodates a simple arrangement of faculty, student and administrative offices with an extended perimeter for exposure to east and west light. The new atrium space creates an interior spatial extension for the existing lobby in order to unify major public areas on three levels of the building. The combined lobby/atrium becomes an informal gathering place for students, faculty, staff and theater patrons. Within the classroom wing, four rooms form a concentrated group of instructional facilities. The placement of the classrooms underground is advantageous, since they are for audiovisual use and should not admit natural light. Furthermore, the use of underground space allows the office wing placed above ground level to be modest in scale.

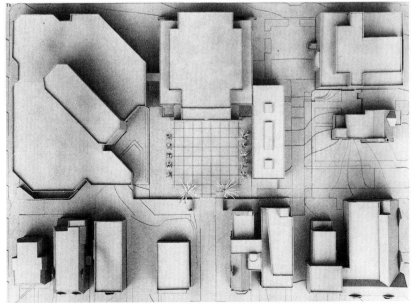

5

WALTER ROYAL DAVIS LIBRARY
University of North Carolina at Chapel Hill
Chapel Hill, North Carolina 1982
With Leslie N. Boney Architect

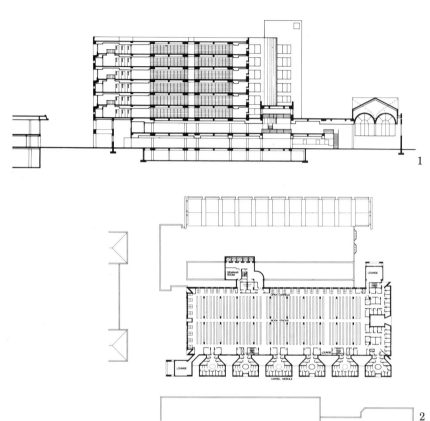

This research library is on a three acre site flanked by three existing campus buildings and the student union. The 438,000 square foot structure contains approximately ten acres of floor space, with a two million volume book capacity, seating for 3,500 readers, approximately 500 closed study carrels and 144 faculty studies. The plan makes a clear distinction between the character of the areas in which a book is stored and those in which it is read. A landscaped brick plaza forms an entrance court to the building, from which the reader passes directly into a three-story gallery space. This lively interior space, illuminated by light wells, provides direct access to book circulation processing, to a periodicals reading room and to a mezzanine from which elevators rise into the book stack floors. These six floors are organized into concentrated book storage in the center, surrounded by open study carrels on the west and north sides, faculty studies on the east side and closed study carrels on the south side. The closed carrels are arranged in six vertical modules and are designed to provide natural light and exterior views for readers working within their spaces. A two-story, double-arched main reading room flanks the entire north side of the building. The airy enclosure of this room, with diffused natural light creates an alive yet serene place appropriate for intense study and reflection.

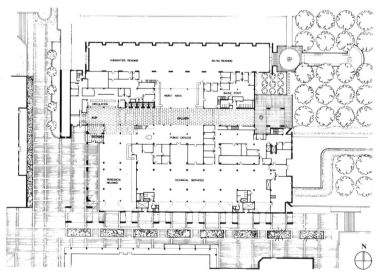

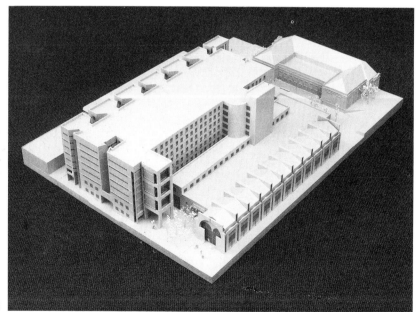

5

6

8

7

1 Section looking west
2 Typical stack floor plan
3 Ground floor plan
4 Model view from the northeast
5 Detail of south facade
6 Reading room looking east
7 Detail of west facade
8 View from the southwest

Bartholomew Consolidated School Corporation
Columbus, Indiana 1973

2

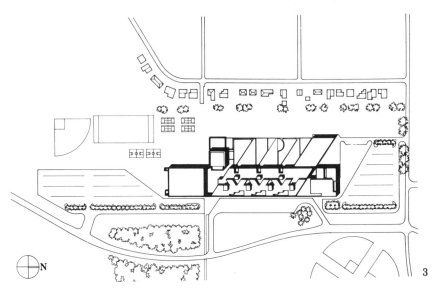

3

This school is built on a flat, L-shaped site of 53 acres in a low density residential area and within a flood plain. The curriculum for the high school is based upon a flexible system which extensively rearranges traditional instructional time blocks. Rather than classroom periods, school time is divided into 15 minute modules which the student arranges to meet his own instructional needs. New methods of instruction utilize a variety of group sizes ranging from independent study to large groups of 450 students. Emphasis is placed on extensive use of technological aids, television and other multimedia devices.

Serving a population of 2,100 students, the building is organized according to a plan for vertical separation of different functions and activity levels. The first floor is the point of arrival and distribution, and is developed along a linear gallery with an exterior plaza at one end flanked by a swimming pool and gymnasium and an auditorium at the other. Various functions are distributed along the gallery, including public and visitor-oriented spaces, lounges or common areas, large group instruction areas and a locker level below. The second floor is an open flexible space for independent study with facilities for scheduled and unscheduled student use including resource materials, books, departmental offices, studios and laboratories. The third floor contains roof decks and 33 seminar spaces for small groups. Construction materials are aluminum "sandwich panel" walls for enclosure of the upper two floors of flexible-use space, and ground floor walls are of glazed structural clay tile over concrete block.

1 Main entrance detail, east elevation
2 East elevation
3 Site plan

4

5

6

7

8

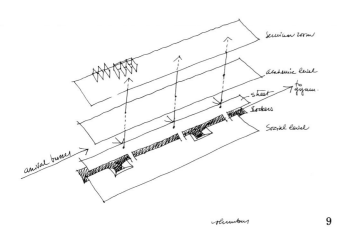

9

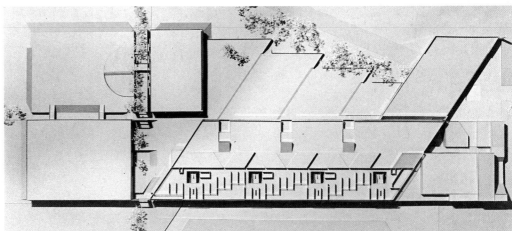

10

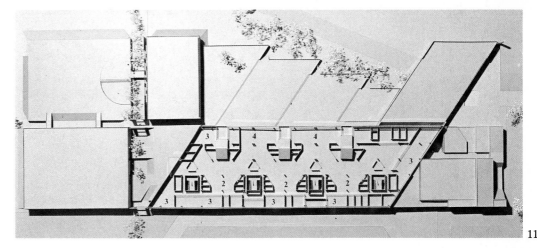

11

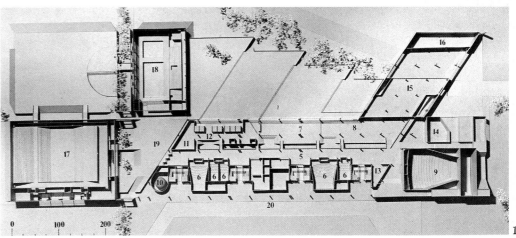

12

1 Sloped aluminum window
2 Insulated aluminum panel
3 Gasket window
4 Continuous light fixture
5 Handrail
6 Wood deck
7 Steel column cover
8 Aluminum soffit

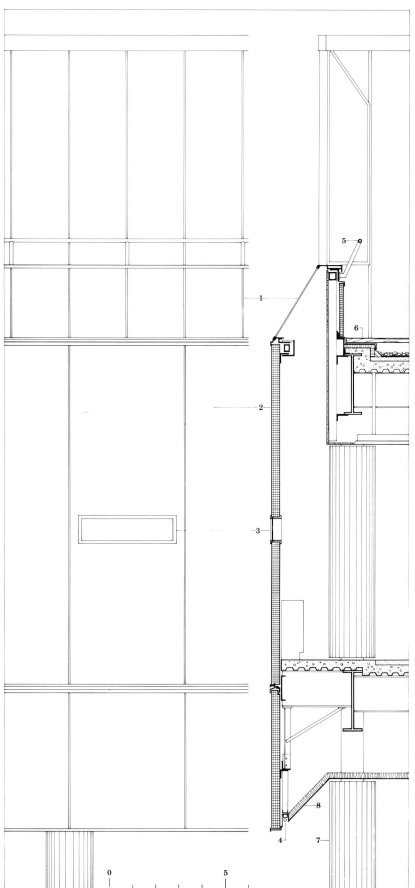

0   5

13

14

15

16

17

18

19

20

21

22

23

24

1

William Penn High School is on Broad Street on a seven acre site close to the center of the city. It serves as a neighborhood school for 3,000 pupils and also houses part of the city's "magnet system" of shared specialized facilities. The specialties accommodated at this high school are in the fields of communications and language. The size of the project and the complexities of a double program articulate and separate the various components of the school into distinct architectural elements. The development of the project as a village of many buildings rather than as a single structure reduces the school's scale into comprehensible parts. The elements are shaped and located according to their size and degree of public utilization. The large single building facing Broad Street is in a scale appropriate to its public facilities and to the civic nature of the street. The student union, administrative offices, theatre and "magnet" specialties are here, and it also contains the main entrance to the school. The characteristic functions of the neighborhood school are accommodated in a series of six smaller scale academic houses, each holding 500 students.

Each "academic house" contains eight flexible classrooms, faculty offices and a two story learning center where 250 semiprivate carrels form a home base for the student. The houses are set within a green area, secluded from the distractions of the street; they are considered as "schools within a school," and are the architectural nucleus of the project. The dining building is at the rear of the site, facing a low density, small scale residential area. The structure is divided into a series of 12 rooms which modulate its size requirements on the inside and provide an exterior scale suitable to the residences beyond. The circulation system ties the elements of the project together. Access is channeled into two main transverse galleries, along one of which is the instructional materials center and library. These galleries are enriched with areas where students may sit and interact on an informal basis. The complexities of the project are unified by a prevailing simplicity of construction materials. Poured-in-place concrete is left as cast both inside and out, and is the primary structural and skin system for all parts of the school.

1 Entrance detail, west facade
2 First level plan
3 East-west section

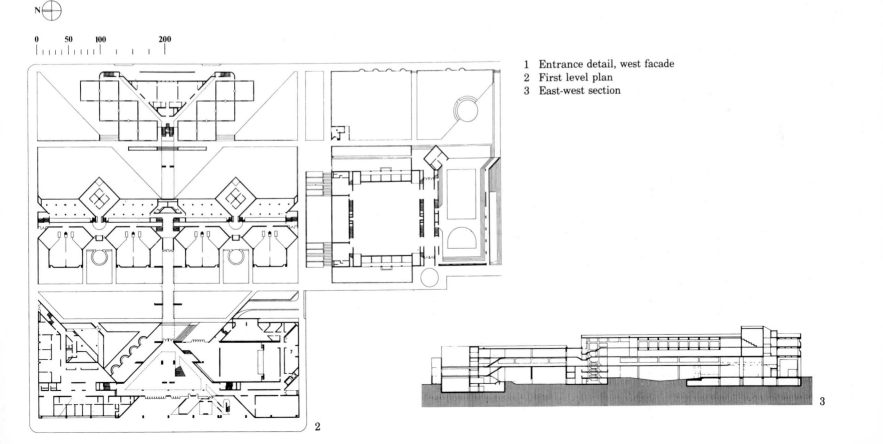

4

5

6

7

8

9

ELEMENTARY SCHOOL
Associazione Nazionale Alpini
U.S. Agency for International Development
Aviano, Italy 1981

1

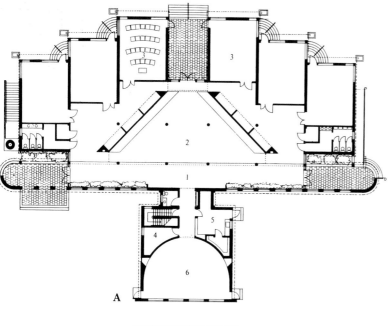

A

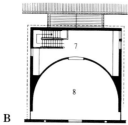

B

2

This elementary school near the town of Aviano was part of a widespread program to revive the Friuli area of northeastern Italy devastated by the earthquakes of 1976. The site borders on a road on the south side, and to the north overlooks broad fields and a chain of mountains in the distance. The program for this school is based on the standard guidelines of the Italian public education system. It consists of six classrooms for 25 pupils each, a main meeting area, a 75-seat dining room/conference space and the necessary support spaces.

The classrooms are grouped around a central meeting place. This centralized plan for the school provides a buffer zone for circulation and coat storage between classrooms and the meeting room, allows each classroom to be oriented in two directions and provides convenient access from each room to the outside. Opposite the central meeting space is a long entry gallery. Exterior porticoes form the entryways at both ends. The dining room and the teacher's mezzanine are partially detached from the general life of the school and are in a central pavilion on the opposite side of the gallery. This double height room is oriented towards the street. Its separation from the rest of the school is further emphasized by the solid semicircular wall on its north side.

The exterior massing and elevations express the different components of the school. The street elevation presents the regular rhythm of the entry gallery which forms a backdrop for the central dining pavilion. This pavilion is articulated on the front facade by a multicolored geometric design composed of various stones and marbles characteristic of northern Italy.

South elevation 1
Ground floor and second floor plan: *1) gallery, 2) meeting room, 3) classroom,* 2
4) office, 5) warm-up kitchen, 6) dining hall, 7) staff room, 8) open to below
Northeast elevation 3

3

4 Northeast entrance
5 Entrance to individual classrooms on north side
6 Dining hall
7 View from the north

8

9

10

11

8 Central meeting room
9 Dining hall
10 Entrance gallery and meeting room
11 South elevation viewed from the road

TECHNICAL HIGH SCHOOL
Associazione Nazionale Alpini
U.S. Agency for International Development
Maniago, Italy 1981

The Technical High School is on the outskirts of Maniago, a small agricultural town in the Friuli region of Italy. With the exception of a few residential buildings near the site, the school's context is dominated by views of the massive mountains to the north. The program for the school was determined by the official guidelines for Italian education standards. The school consists of 19 classrooms, an auditorium, library, gymnasium, dining hall, custodian's apartment, administration offices and support spaces. The design is organized around a system of courts linked by a central circulation and service spine. This plan provides a variety of spaces with differing characters, preventing a sense of institutional monotony. The horizontal extension of the plan also reduces the mass of the building, allowing it to be compatible with the surrounding houses. Because the architectural scale of the complex is graduated according to function, spaces are created which range from accommodation of large groups to small areas appropriate for more personal or individual use. Porticoes and arcades also allow outside activities and access to fresh air even during inclement weather.

East elevation 1
Entrance 2
Detail of north elevation 3
Central court, looking northeast 4
Site plan 5
Ground floor plan 6
Detail of entrance 7
Central court, looking east 8

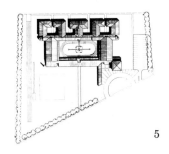

5

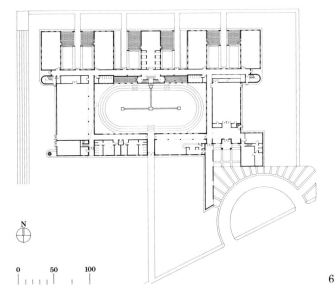

N

0 50 100

6

7

8

198

9

10

11

12

STUDENT HOUSING

Associazione Nazionale Alpini
U.S. Agency for International Development
San Pietro al Natisone, Italy 1981

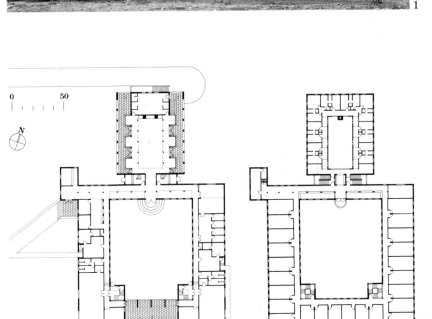

This student hostel is in a small town in Italy near the Yugoslavian border, and is on a site at the edge of a long valley nestled in the mountains. The town of San Pietro al Natisone contains several schools and a teacher's college. The hostel provides housing five days a week for students at San Pietro's schools who come from distant rural areas, and who only return home on weekends. The two story hostel consists of a square courtyard enclosed by the dormitory, public rooms and an adjoining building housing the single bedrooms and dining hall. The architecture conveys a sense of a "home away from home" for students accustomed to the strong domestic traditions of rural areas. A focal point in the building is a large fireplace in the dining hall, which functions as a gathering place for the students who can view the mountains where their families live. The large central court is similar to the traditional farmyard yet also has the formal appearance of an urban setting reflecting the sense of a communal institution.

1 View from the north
2 Site plan
3 Ground floor plan
4 Second floor plan
5 Entrance
6 View from the south

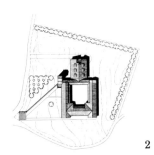

7 Gallery
8 Dining hall detail
9 Southeast view from courtyard through portico
10 Northwest view from portico to courtyard
11 Dining hall

7

8

9

10

Urban places emerge from the collective proximity of different land uses, as in the juxtaposition of this college with its residences and the city's Main Street.

Central Business District Plan
Wilkes-Barre
Pennsylvania
1967

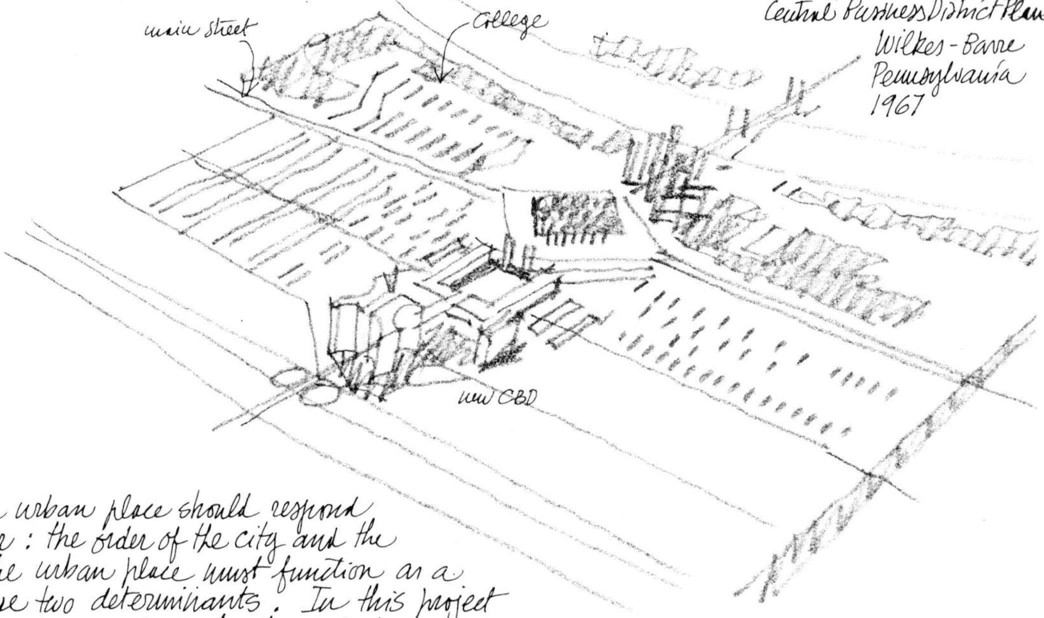

N.Y. Trade Center

main street

College

new CBD

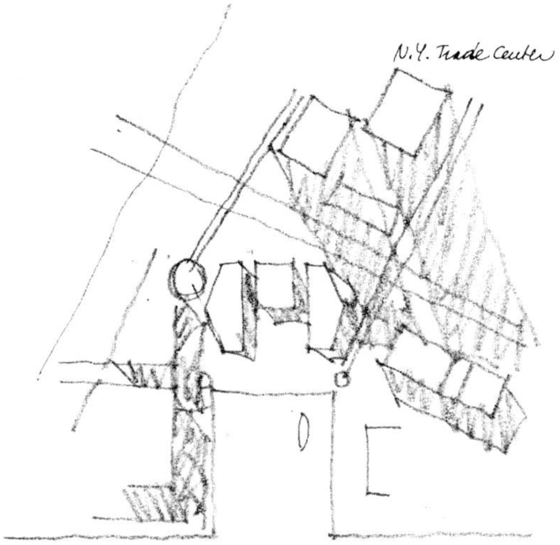

Hudson River

Battery Park Development
New York, New York
competition 1982

Like a building, an urban place should respond to two kinds of order: the order of the city and the order of nature. The urban place must function as a bridge between these two determinants. In this project some of the buildings are ordered by the waterfront, others by the geometry of the city.

The architecture of this building forming the edge between the commercial and the monumental districts in Washington D.C. intends to reflect both the ideals of private initiative and the order of the public place.

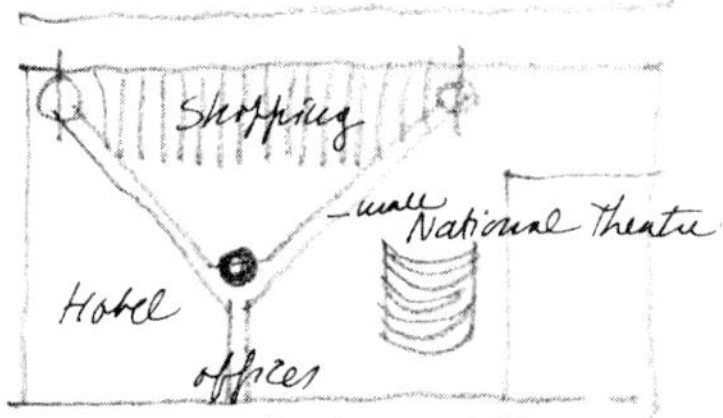

Shopping

mall   National Theatre

Hotel

offices

National Place
Hotel-offices-Retail
Complex
Washington D.C. 1983
(w. Frank Schlesinger
FAIA architect,
Planners)

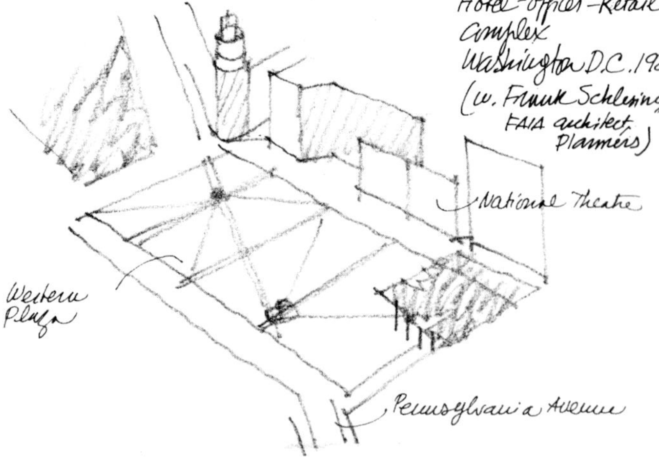

National Theatre

Western
Plaza

Pennsylvania Avenue

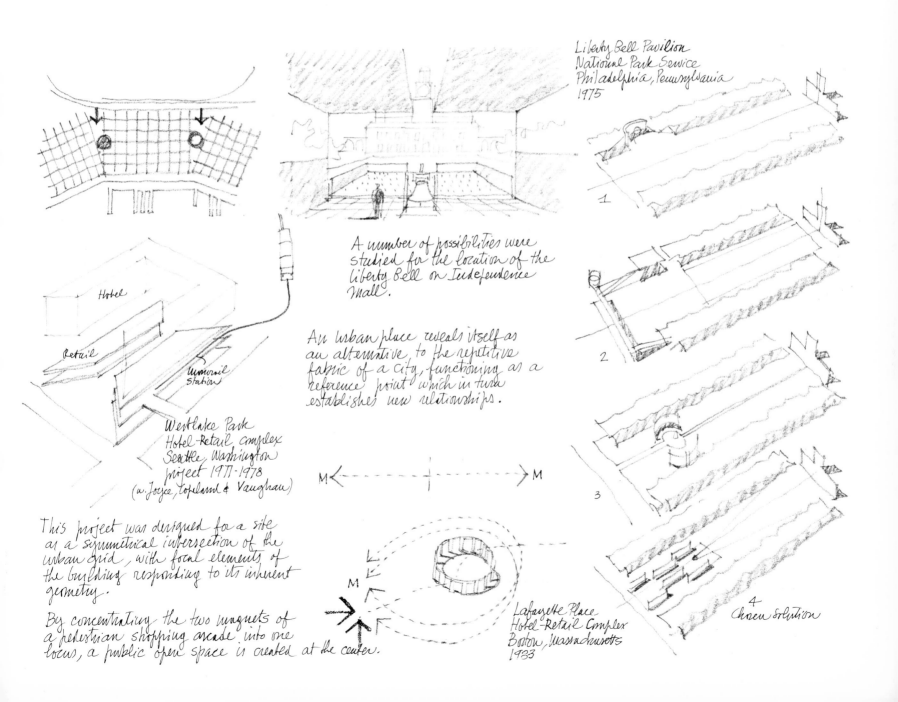

Liberty Bell Pavilion
National Park Service
Philadelphia, Pennsylvania
1975

A number of possibilities were
studied for the location of the
Liberty Bell on Independence
Mall.

An urban place reveals itself as
an alternative to the repetitive
fabric of a city, functioning as a
reference point which in turn
establishes new relationships.

1

2

3

4
Chosen Solution

Hotel

Retail

Memorial
Station

Westlake Park
Hotel-Retail Complex
Seattle, Washington
project 1971-1978
(w. Joyce, Copeland & Vaughan)

This project was designed for a site
as a symmetrical intersection of the
urban grid, with focal elements of
the building responding to its inherent
geometry.

By concentrating the two magnets of
a pedestrian shopping arcade into one
locus, a public open space is created at the center.

Lafayette Place
Hotel-Retail Complex
Boston, Massachusetts
1933

ROMA INTERROTTA EXHIBITION
Incontri Internazionali d'Arte
Rome, Italy 1978

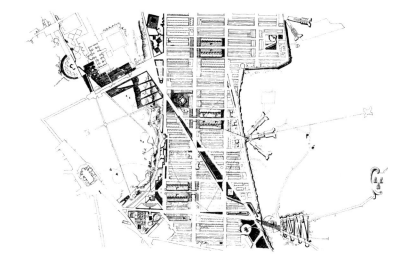

1

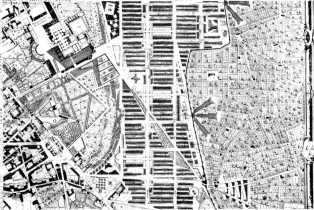

2

In the autumn of 1978, an exhibition entitled "Roma Interrotta" was held in the Markets of Trajan in Rome. The exhibition was the culmination of a year-long project in which 12 architects were each assigned a sector of Giambattista Nolli's city plan of Rome, completed in 1748, and were asked to design an imaginary "intervention" within the plan.

The intervention or solution produced by the Mitchell/Giurgola design team for Nolli's Sector VI can best be described by excerpts quoted from the design's original project statement:

The Aurelian Wall becomes the generator of new urban structures. Within it there will be the development of an active life of labor and trade. Along those walls people build their own houses, buildings for public use, workshops, markets, schools and places for recreation. . . . The walls, which do not have to defend anyone any longer, feed the city. Within them, computerized pipelines have been built to feed food and materials needed by the markets and the workshops uninterruptedly along the perimeter of the whole city. . . . Near the San Lorenzo gate there is a building of initiation: at the same time an inn and a school; a place where anyone who wishes to immigrate to the city stops for a period to learn something about the city within the walls, prepare himself for that life. . . . The framework of that ancient city is solid and within it the problems are solved in the traditional fashion. To the east outside the wall, work is harmonized with the natural cycles. In the space between the two ancient walls the process of life transforms the area, and questions are posed over and over again.

1 Site analysis
2 New plan superimposed on old plan
3 Sketch plan
4 The Aurelian Wall feeding the city
5 Section of the park
6 Sketch of the park

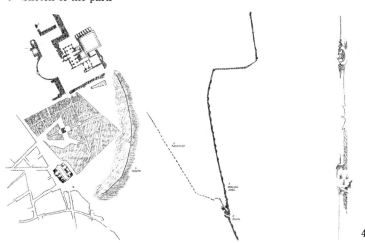

3

4

SUBWAY CONCOURSE ENTRANCE
City of Philadelphia
Philadelphia, Pennsylvania 1971

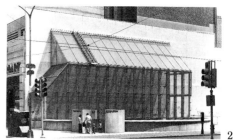

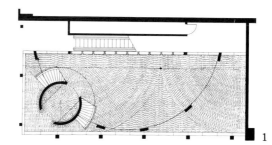

1   Plan at concourse level
2   Street level view from the northwest
3   Concourse level view from the south

MARKET STREET EAST DEVELOPMENT
Philadelphia City Planning Commission
Philadelphia, Pennsylvania 1962

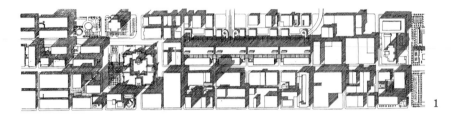

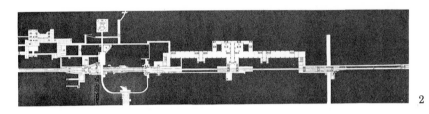

1 Site plan
2 Concourse level plan
3 Section perspective

208

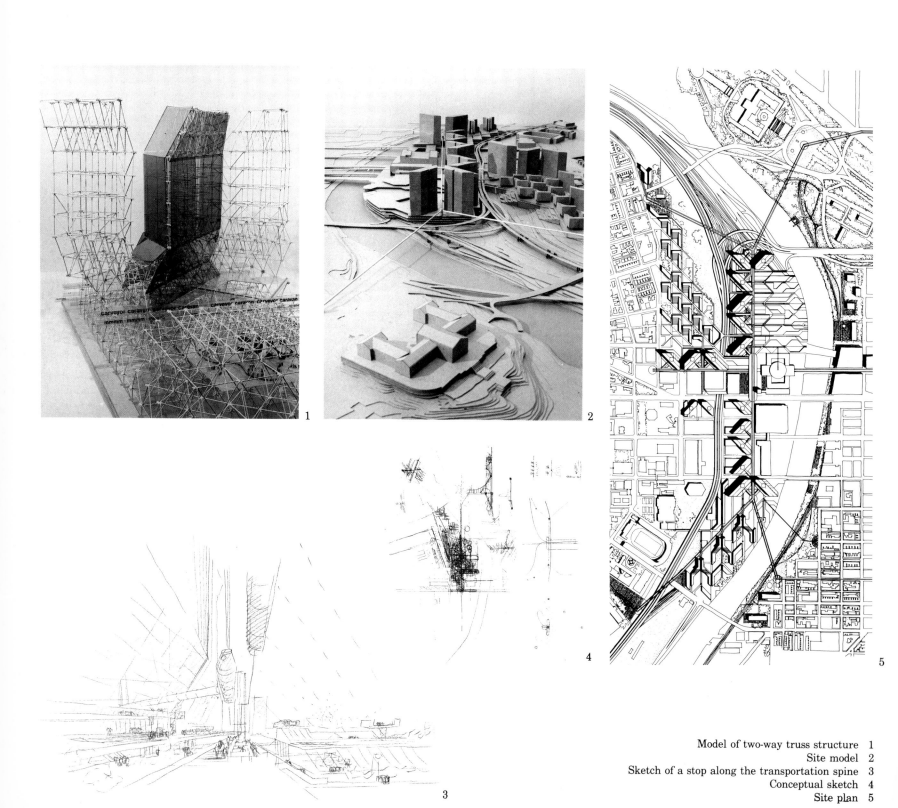

Model of two-way truss structure 1
Site model 2
Sketch of a stop along the transportation spine 3
Conceptual sketch 4
Site plan 5

30TH STREET SITE MASTER PLAN
EASTWICK SITE MASTER PLAN
The Philadelphia 1976 Bicentennial Corporation
Philadelphia, Pennsylvania
1970 with David Crane
1972 with the offices of Louis I. Kahn; Venturi and Rauch;
Bower and Fradley; Murphy, Levy, Wurman; and Eshbach
Glass, Kale & Associates

As a consultant to the City Planning Commission, Romaldo Giurgola was involved in the Market Street East project for development of new retail and office areas in conjunction with new suburban rail facilities. The primary planning principle was to reinforce Market Street as a continuous architectural experience serving as a strong connective link between Independence Mall and City Hall at the city's center. By introducing a continuous multilevel, skylit pedestrian mall parallel to Market Street, retail shops maintain a dual frontage for access to both pedestrian areas, and congestion on Market Street is reduced. The plan integrates major transportation systems, and offices, hotels and residential facilities are also connected to the mall.

The 30th Street Site Master Plan proposed development of the air rights above the railroad yards adjacent to Center City, with office, residential, retail and convention facilities planned for inauguration at the time of the 1976 Bicentennial. The Eastwick Site Master Plan represents one aspect of a jointly prepared planning proposal in which a World Fair facility for the bicentennial was developed around the concept of a central "street" flanked on both sides by pavilions.

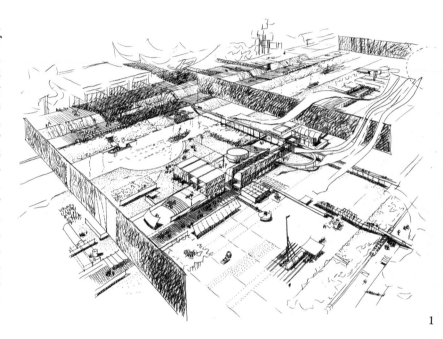

1

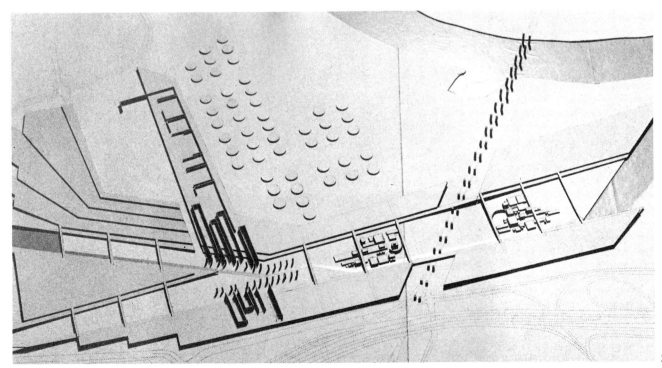

1 Aerial view sketch
2 Site model

2

COLUMBIA AVENUE STATION IMPROVEMENTS
City of Philadelphia and Temple University
Philadelphia, Pennsylvania 1984

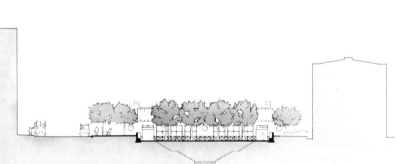

1

The subway station at the corner of Broad and Columbia Streets serves thousands of students who commute daily to Temple University. In addition, this intersection is a major cross axis for general city public transport. Before initiation of this project, no amenities existed above ground for use by this large commuter population, and an adjacent vacant lot was traversed diagonally by students to reach the north/south pedestrian access within the university grounds. In order to enhance this bleak yet vital area, the project increases the capacity of the existing subway station, develops an "entrance" to the university from the subway's orientation, and constructs a "stair building" or pavilion above the subway stairs flanked by a landscaped plaza. The "stair building" gives the subway an identity as a focal point on the street and its outer wall also separates the plaza from the noise of Broad Street traffic. The lower court of the "stair building" permits sunlight to enter the subway spaces and allows views from the subway platform into the trees above. The character and detailing of the original subway station, built in 1924, is preserved wherever possible. The simple rectangular plaza flanking the "stair building" complements but does not emphasize the diagonal movement of students toward the campus. Paving, perimeter seating, sculpture and a central bosque of evergreen holly trees define the sense of place in the plaza. Planting around its perimeter enhances its character of transparent enclosure, making it a place of oasis within the surrounding urban atmosphere for local residents, commuters and students.

2

3

4

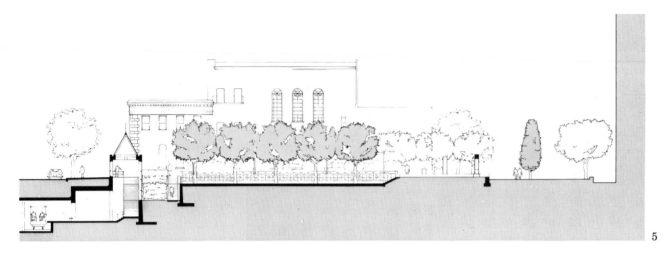

5

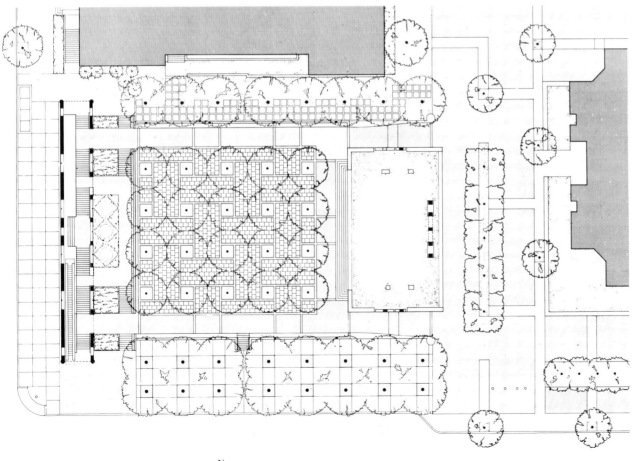

0   10   50   N

6

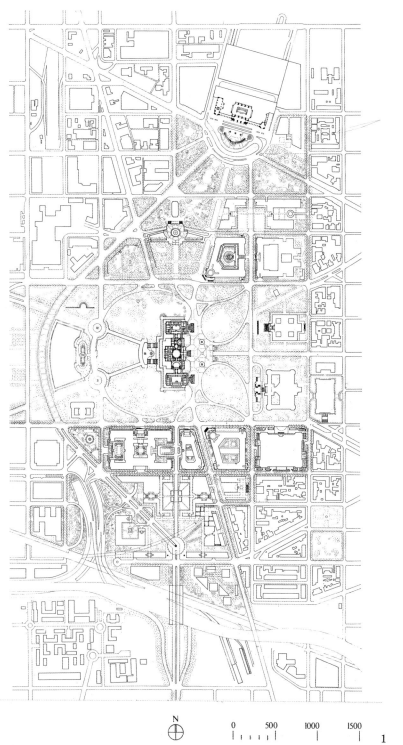

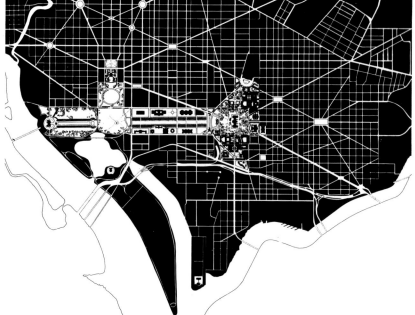

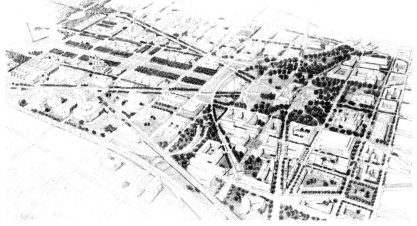

N

0   500   1000   1500

1

Ground level plan of master plan, from north to south: *Union Station,* 1
Senate Office buildings, Capitol, House Office Buildings

Capitol grounds and mall 2

Capitol grounds and mall from the southeast 3

Diagrams from top to bottom: *Capitol and government building framework,* 4
Capitol and Senate office buildings, Capitol and House office buildings,
Capitol and greenspace

Future Senate office buildings and plaza 5

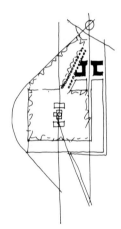

UNITED STATES CAPITOL MASTER PLAN FOR THE FUTURE DEVELOPMENT OF THE CAPITOL GROUNDS AND RELATED AREAS
Architect of the Capitol
Washington, D.C. 1977-1981
Design Consultant with Wallace, Roberts and Todd

In July 1975, the U.S. Congress directed the Architect of the Capitol to prepare a master plan for future development of the United States Capitol grounds. During the subsequent five years until submission of the plan to Congress in October 1981, Mitchell/Giurgola Architects served as the consultant for architecture to the Architect of the Capitol on this project. This study, which furnishes Congress with a complete master plan for the next 50 to 75 years of development on Capitol Hill, includes an assessment of the existing urban fabric; planning for future building locations; analysis of open space utilization, traffic and transportation systems; and a study of the relationship between the government sector and the surrounding historic district.

This project was understood not merely as an exercise in efficient planning and development, but rather as a search for a plan responding to the complex contemporary aspiration for a humane urban environment. In consequence, each aspect of the plan was studied in detail within the framework of several contexts: its symbolism or meaning, its historical context and its physical form.

Mitchell/Giurgola Architects' responsibilities included the analysis of existing buildings and districts on Capitol Hill; conceptual design and planning of new sectors for buildings and open spaces; preparation of plans, drawings and renderings for presentation and publication; and the writing and editing of major parts of the final master plan document submitted to Congress.

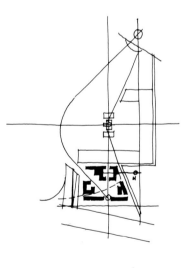

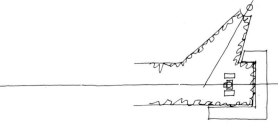

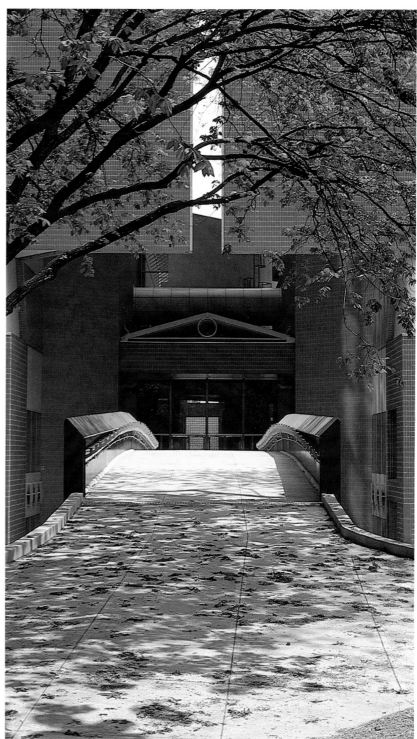

STRAWBERRY SQUARE
Harristown Development Corporation
Harrisburg, Pennsylvania 1979
With Lawrie and Green

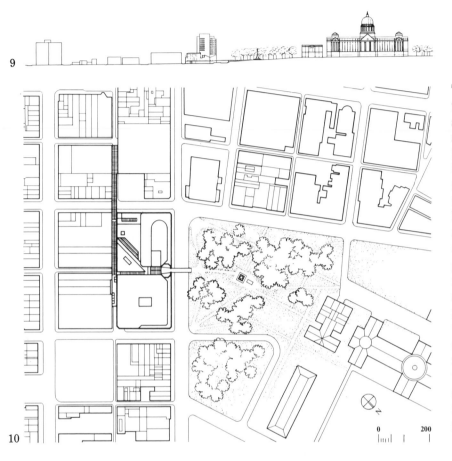

This complex of office and commercial space is a pivotal element in the urban renewal of downtown Harrisburg. Included within the structure are two office towers of unequal size, a department store, shops, restaurants, garage and service facilities and a public gathering place. The complex is at the edge of the park containing the state Capitol, and major administrative offices of the Commonwealth. The new building is intended to present a strong frontage to the park in the tradition of many American townscapes. The difference in size between the two office towers has been reconciled through the use of a uniform cornice, 12 stories high, which recalls the general height of other buildings surrounding the park. The presence of the public gathering place between the two buildings in the complex is announced at the entrance by a vertical slot in the elevation. Below this aperture is a sunny entrance court from which the vistor may proceed into the retail areas, enter the lobbies of the two principal office tenants or enter the public gathering place. This triangular room is quiet in attitude, acting as a foil for the visual activities of the commercial spaces beyond. Facade materials are matte red and grey tile with polished granite trim. The nine story office elevation reflects the scale and characteristic red color of city buildings, while the setback facade changes to a regressive coloration of light grey, recalling the grey limestone Capitol.

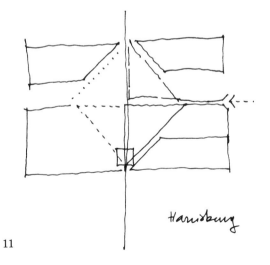

Harrisburg

6 Detail of facade above main entry
7 Entrance lobby
8 Detail of main entry
9 City section
10 Site plan
11 Conceptual sketch
12 Northeast elevation

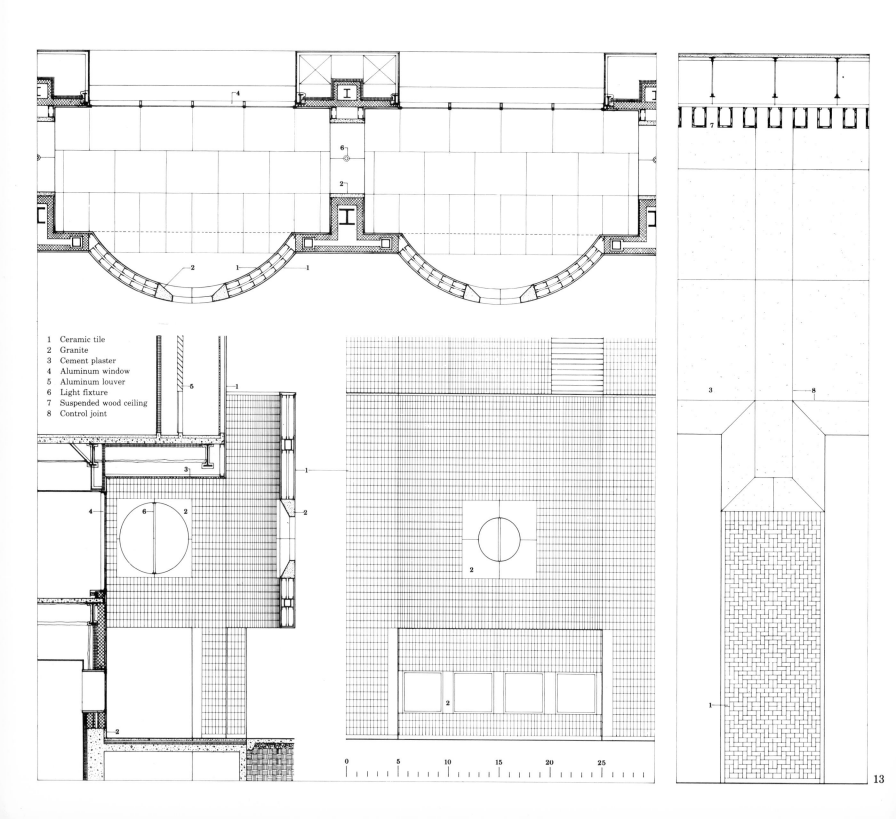

1 Ceramic tile
2 Granite
3 Cement plaster
4 Aluminum window
5 Aluminum louver
6 Light fixture
7 Suspended wood ceiling
8 Control joint

0   5   10   15   20   25

13

13 Interior and exterior tile wall details
14 Interior detail of facade window
15 Atrium with gazebo
16 Retail shops in atrium

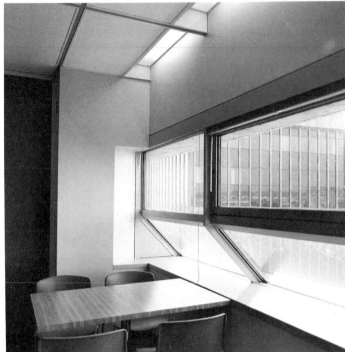
14

16

15

17

18

19

20

21

22

WESTLAKE PARK, PHASE I AND II
Mondev International Limited
Seattle, Washington 1977, 1980
1977 with Joyce Copeland Vaughn and Nordfors
1980 with Joyce/Nordfors and Associates

Sketch of southeast entry 1
Site plan 2
Street level plan 3

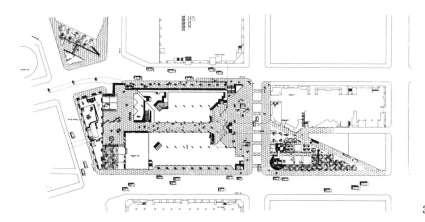

The Westlake Park project is a joint public and private development at the heart of Seattle's retail core. Surrounded by the city's three major department stores, the site also contains the terminus of the monorail that connects the Seattle Fairgrounds to the downtown area. In its first phase of development, the project extends the concept of a city recreational space through an itinerary of landscaped areas and an enclosed shopping arcade into a major paved plaza for public gatherings, uniting the disparate properties adjacent to the site into an urban whole. According to this plan, the terminus for the monorail, underground parking and three levels of retail shops support a new low rise hotel constructed around a pool and a series of gardens.

In the project's second phase, proposals for relocation of the Seattle Art Museum on the upper two floors of the complex were included in the redesign of the plan. At the south end of the building, landscaped roof terraces step down toward a triangular urban park. The two low terraces are easily accessible to the public, and the top sculpture terrace is reserved for museum visitors.

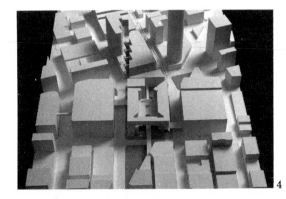

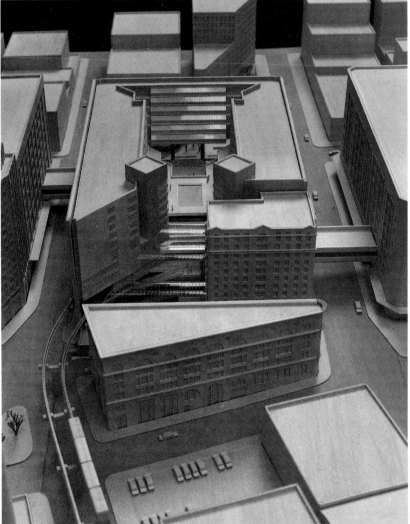

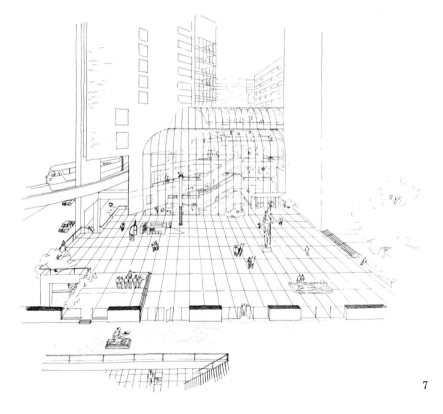

Site study model 4
Southwest plaza and entry 5
View from the northwest showing transit connection 6
Sketch of north plaza 7

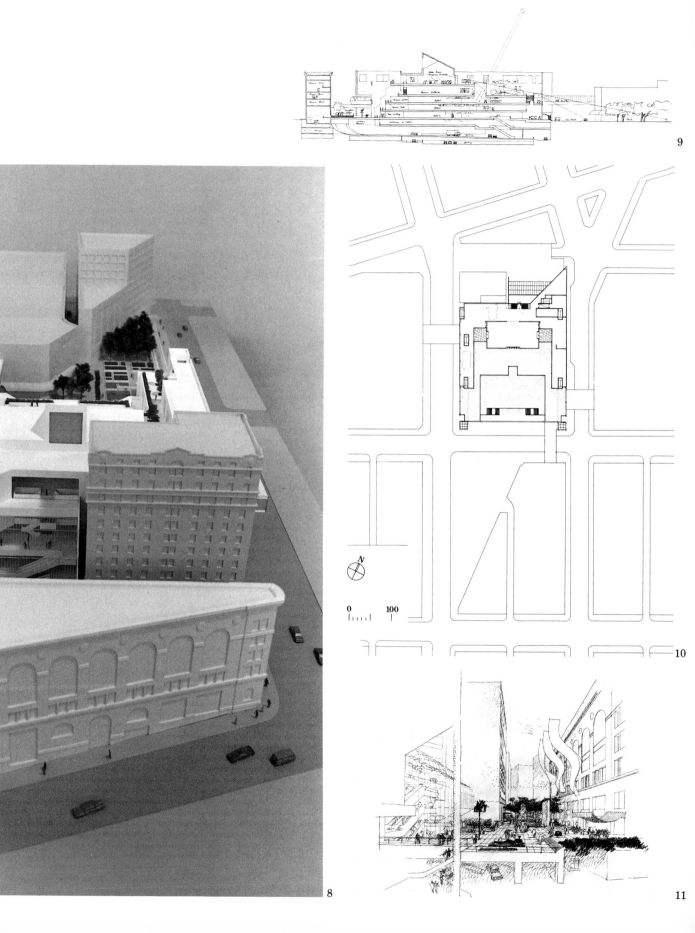

9

8

10

11

12

NATIONAL PLACE
Square 254 Limited Partnership
Washington, D.C. 1983
With Frank Schlesinger Architects/Planners

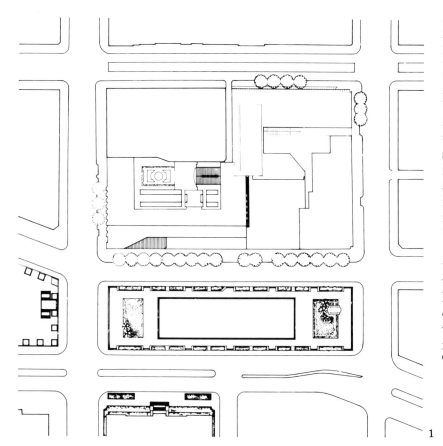

National Place is a mixed use building which includes a Marriott hotel, commercial offices, retail space and parking. The project is located in downtown Washington, D.C. in an area of intense urban renewal activity along Pennsylvania Avenue. The National Place site acts as a bridge between the symbolic and monumental aspects of Washington (typified by Western Plaza, the federal building complex and the Mall to the south) and the more everyday life of the community represented by the commercial area to the north. In addition, the site functions as an important link in the large scale "chain" connecting Capitol Hill with the White House and the Treasury Building. At a more immediate scale, development on the site must be carefully related to the Willard Hotel and the National Theater. The theater is of significance to the National Place design, functioning as the "seed" or starting point for the building's form.

The particular sense of presence of the building is produced by a unique aspect of the design. Mixed use projects are usually designed to "stack" different uses in horizontal layers. Within the National Place complex, the offices and hotel are also layered vertically, with office space overlooking Pennsylvania Avenue flanked by hotel rooms which face a large, open interior courtyard. This design allows accommodation of all of the major tenants—the hotel, offices and National Theater—on the prime but restricted avenue frontage.

1

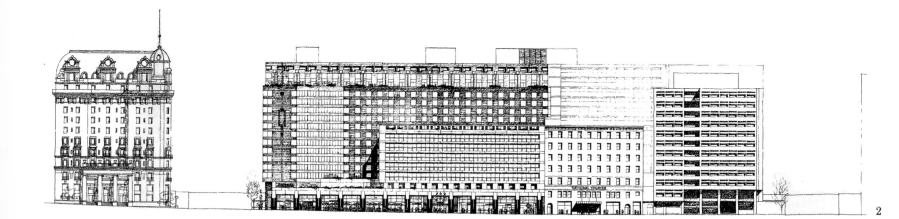

2

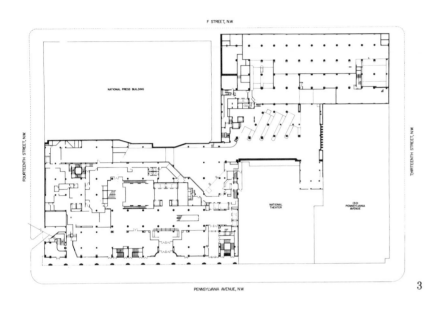

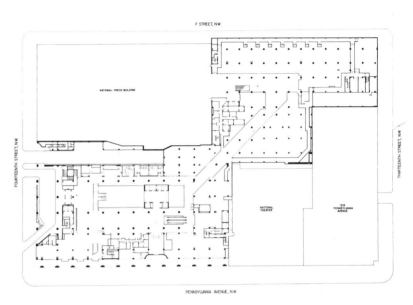

1 Site plan
2 Pennsylvania Avenue elevation
3 Street level plan: *retail, restaurant, parking*
4 Hotel lobby plan: *main entry, lobby, retail*
5 Site model

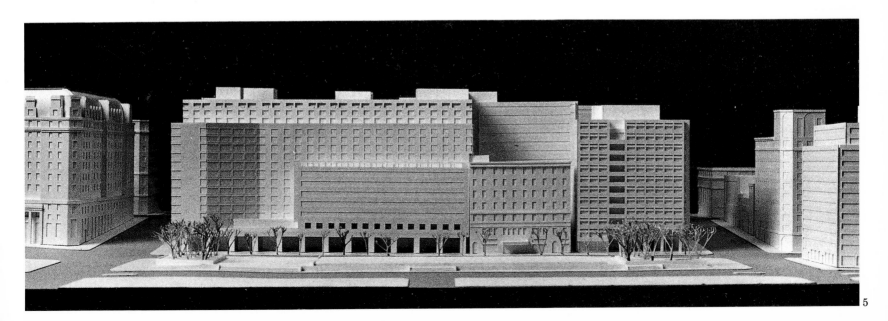

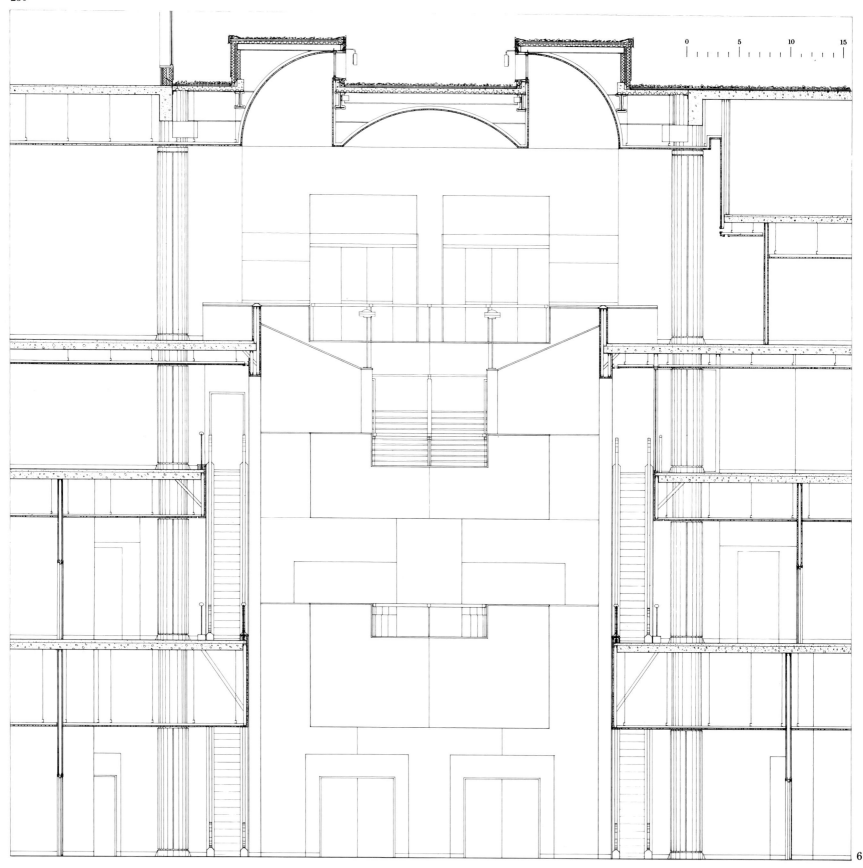

7

6 Section detail through lobby atrium
7 Sketch of Pennsylvania Avenue elevation

1 Site model
2 Model view looking west
3 Axonometric view of site
1 4 Level one plan

LAFAYETTE PLACE
Lafayette Place Associates
Boston, Massachusetts 1983

2

Lafayette Place is a mixed use complex composed of public spaces and private uses especially conceived to enhance and complement each other. The building is an air-rights structure above a municipal underground garage. Three separate elements—retail space, a public plaza and a 500 room hotel—have been integrated into a single structure. European shopping arcades, such as those of Paris and London with their relatively narrow passages, ground floor shops and continuous show windows, are the point of departure for the retail organization of Lafayette Place. Retail space is divided between two levels of similar design where shopfronts define both sides of a curvilinear pedestrian passage. At the south side of the site, the passages connect with a public outdoor courtyard which is a focus for the entire project. On the second level, enclosed terraces with cafes and restaurants surround and overlook the court. At the north end of the site, the arcades connect with the Jordan Marsh department store on both levels. At the third level, additional retail shops and the public areas of the hotel are organized around the central courtyard. The hotel tower rises 22 stories on the southeast corner of the site, affording views of the waterfront and Beacon Hill. Guest room floors are accessible through a series of superimposed four-story atria. The triangular arrival lounge spaces at the southern end of the linear plan open onto terraces with views toward the southwest.

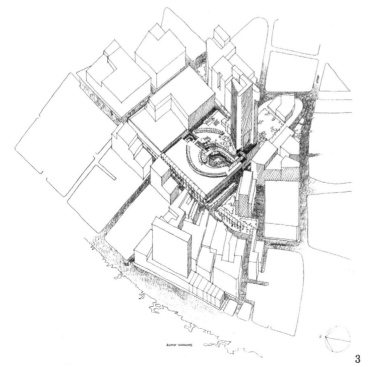

3

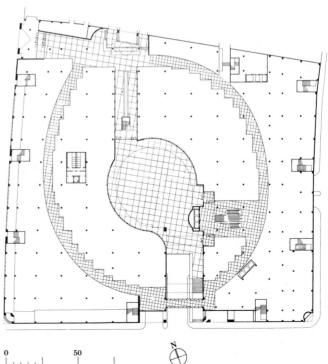

0   50

4

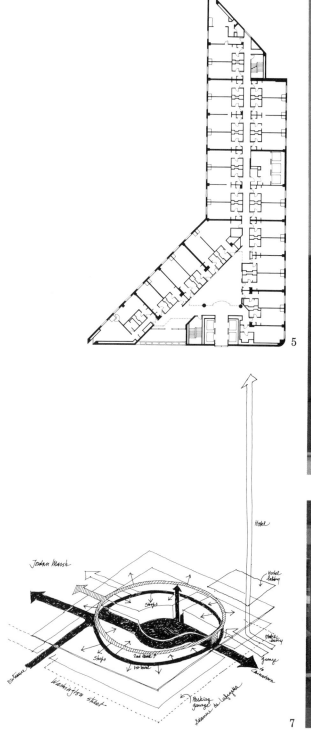

5

6

7

8

9

10

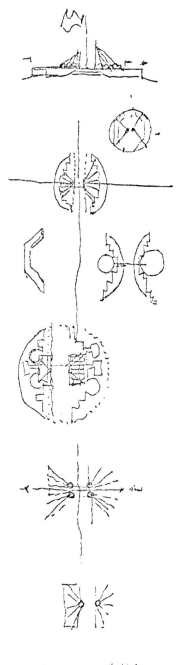

Site model view looking northeast 1
Conceptual sketches 2

2

In June 1980, the Australian Parliament House Construction Authority announced that the joint entry of Mitchell/Giurgola Architects and Richard Thorp, an Australian architect, had won first prize from among 329 entries in the international competition for the design of Australia's new Parliament House. Located in Canberra, the Parliament building complex will be a structure of approximately 1,500,000 square feet, with a total budget of 220 million Australian dollars (May 1978 prices). Construction began in November 1981, with a projected completion date of June 1988. A new office, Mitchell/Giurgola & Thorp Architects, has been established in Canberra to carry out this project.

The site, established by the 1912 Griffin Plan and the 1974 Parliament Act, is a rounded hill in Canberra. The design accepts the circular site of the hill as the generating form of the Parliament complex. Within that circle, a central, linear sequence of formal meeting rooms is framed by two massive curvilinear walls which enclose within their arcs the Offices and Chambers of the Senate and House of Representatives. As a result the entire complex has four major elements: the Senate, the House of Representatives, a central "forum" and a separate Executive Government area. The exterior form of the building follows the natural profile of the hill and is surrounded by landscaped gardens and bosques containing recreational facilities and parking. At the apex of the complex the flag of Australia is supported by a mast structure arising from the building. Thus the general character of the architecture conveys the sense of a balanced, horizontal "nesting" of buildings in a natural setting.

Excerpts from the original text submitted as part of the competition entry in 1980 best describe the general intent and philosophy of the design:

.... our intention in the Canberra design is to arrive at an architectural imprint that derives its value through a balanced and unforgettable geometry. The character of our search for that geometry is in many ways an extension of the spirit infusing the Griffin plan: a plan of intense order and geometric form, but one which results in a pliable and enfolding landscape. This interplay between geometry and softened forms exists not as a contradiction, but rather as a visual imposition. Thus, the spirit of the plan is one of a ceaseless attempt to find a balance, a kind of discourse between organizing geometry and livability, which results in a truly usable space. Our design is based upon four fundamental perceptual principles:

— We consider the land axis of Canberra as the fundamental gesture of the city, a line around which all other design has evolved in circular and radial directions.

— The site, established by the Griffin plan and the Parliament Act of 1974, is at the converging point of primary avenues which connect the area to major points of the city. We interpret this fact as a determination to extend the formal areas of the capital and to form a bridge with the residential sectors of the city.

— The circular site was accepted as the generating form of the Parliament complex. In consequence, our attention has been focused upon a tridimensional system of forms that articulates the basic circular plan without opposing it.

— Our preoccupation as architects has been that of grafting meaning, myths and symbols into a geometric scheme for the Parliament as a synthesis of the nation's presence.

Our concept of the building is not as a monumental structure imposed on the landscape, but rather one which is closer in spirit to the Greek monumentalization of an acropolis, in which there is a continuity from the most minute elements of the architectural order to the massive form of the building itself, yet all of which is congruent with the landscape. We are aware that in any architectural design of this magnitude there is a sense of grandiosity. But it is our intention in the development of the design to resist this connotation of the architectural gesture, and instead to nurture and refine the simple sense of monumentality, in concert with the honest, natural landscape.

.... The form of the Parliament is thus intended to express a sense of fellowship and dignity amongst the citizens, an integrity made evident by the delicate insertion of the complex into the spatial scheme of the city as a whole. Through the buildings' humane accommodation of daily work, and the visual evidence of the commitment of the Government and the dimension of the Commonwealth, the Parliament complex expresses the belief that this fellowship and dignity is not accessorial, but must be conceived of as fundamental to democratic life. (*Stage Two Competition Report*, pp. 4-6, 13)

3

4

5

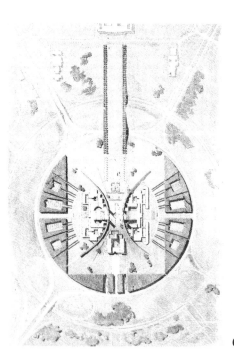

6

7

3 Conceptual city sketch
4 Walter Burley Griffin city plan of 1911
5 City plan with New Parliament House
6 Site plan
7 Forecourt and great verandah screen
  wall

8 First floor plan: *forecourt, verandah,
  foyer, reception hall, members' hall,
  committee and cabinet rooms, executive
  suites, Senate chamber and offices,
  House chamber and offices*
9 Second floor plan: *public terrace, dining
  and gallery, committee rooms, Senate
  offices, House offices*
10 Third floor plan: *Members' terrace and
   dining, library, Senate offices, House
   offices*
11 Model view looking southwest
12 Model view looking toward House
   offices
13 Transverse section through House
   chamber, Members' hall and Senate
   chamber

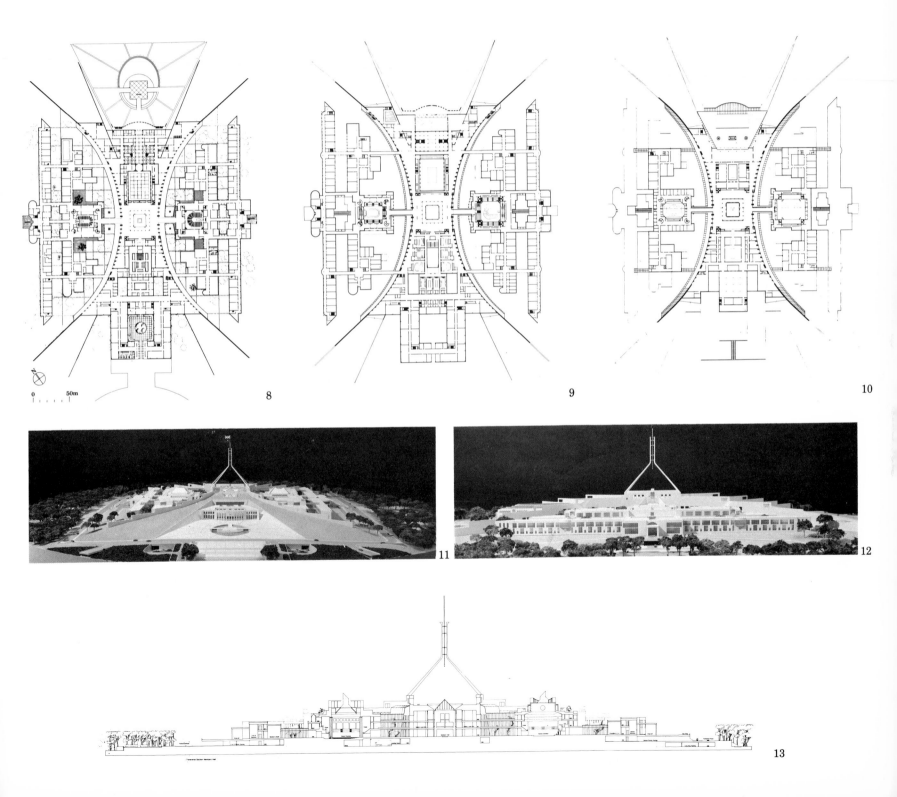

8

9

10

0   50m

11

12

13

16

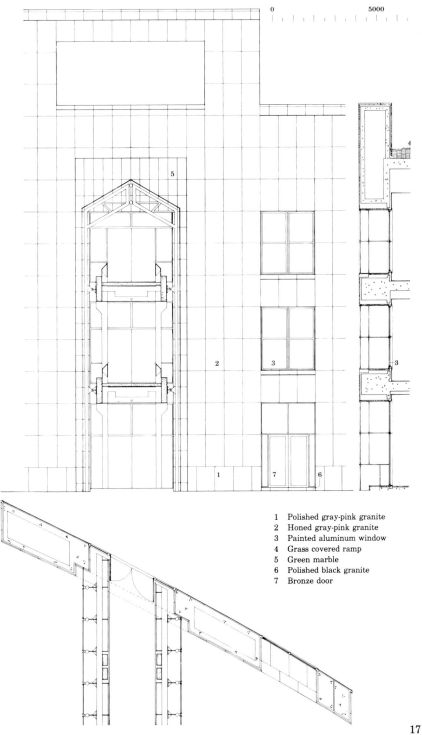

0   5000

18

19

1 Polished gray-pink granite
2 Honed gray-pink granite
3 Painted aluminum window
4 Grass covered ramp
5 Green marble
6 Polished black granite
7 Bronze door

17

20

21

22

The design of the interior spaces of the Parliament is based upon the principle that the success of the design depends upon immediate comprehension by the building's users of its essential simplicity. For this reason, all ceremonial, public and "common" areas are located in a linear sequence along the central zone, while the two chambers lie across from each other on the east-west axis, with their support areas and offices grouped around them. These interior spaces signify their use as a symbolic sequence of rooms of diverse characters. This sequence is functional not only for members of Parliament but also for visitors. The public is allowed to move freely within the ceremonial part of the building and to visit each of the major working areas of the Parliament; this system engenders in the visitor a sense of involvement in the activity of the democratic system.

The symbolic sequence of spaces begins with the forecourt, where formal and festive occasions will be celebrated. The vista from the forecourt down the mall toward the city serves as an initiation to the entire building by creating an implicit reminder of the meaning of what takes place within. From the forecourt the visitor proceeds to the great verandah, which will be a bustling place of transition with constant movement. Beyond the verandah is the foyer, which functions as a monumental space intentionally divided by columns into small bays in which a variety of activities may take place simultaneously. In this way the space can at once establish the grand scale of the building, respond functionally to large crowds and also provide the intimacy necessary to allow individual conversation or quiet reflection.

From the foyer the interior volume of the building opens in two directions: toward the upper floor along an itinerary planned for the public, and ahead into the reception hall along a processional itinerary for members or official visitors. The reception hall will be used for a variety of formal banquets and receptions and must be capable of adaptation both for festive and solemn occasions. Galleries for the public overlook the hall behind a set of lacquered columns, between which tapestries may be hung on special occasions.

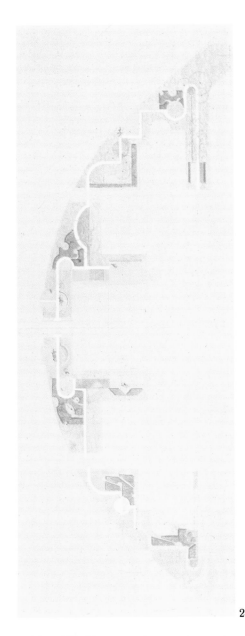

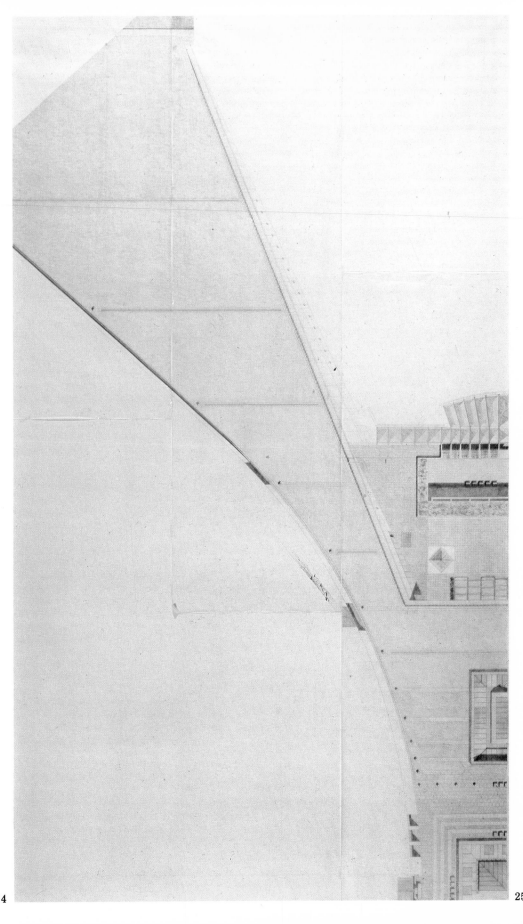

24

25

26

27

28

The Members' Hall is a lofty space at the center of the building delineated on all four sides by simple white plastered portals. The floor is of dark granite, punctuated with a central pool of water reflecting the constant movement of clouds above the glass roof. Skylit glazed passages connect the central spaces with the chambers. The two chambers have different floor plans and architectural configurations. The House Chamber is larger than the Senate, and will be capable of accommodating future joint sessions of both Houses. The differing character of the two chambers will also be defined through the use of fine craftsmanship in woodwork and specially woven and dyed fabrics. Public galleries overlook the Senate and House Chambers and the committee rooms, with soundproof visitors' galleries provided on the second floor level for use as an integral part of the guided public tour of the building.

The offices of Senators and Representatives surround the respective chambers and are designed to provide optimum working conditions. Their arrangement is as non-institutional as possible, with low buildings, generous daylight in working areas in concert with sun control, ample courts and gardens and a potential for expansion and change. The Executive Government sector is located in the southern part of the central zone of the building between the two curved walls. Executive quarters are grouped around a large courtyard designed to permit vehicular entry on special occasions. The suite of offices for the Prime Minister is the focus of the design of spaces surrounding the courtyard, with adjacent suites for the Deputy Leader and other ministers spread over two levels.

The landscaping of the site retains the original character of Capital Hill, with views remaining open between the site and the surrounding city. In conceptual terms, the grounds immediately surrounding the building are treated as a "carpet" consisting of a mixture of manicured lawn and various pavings. The major access road surrounding the Parliament acts as a boundary between the more formal and informal aspects of the landscaping. The perimeter area will be bordered by dense forests of native eucalyptus and acacia trees, cut away to enclose recreational areas and parking.

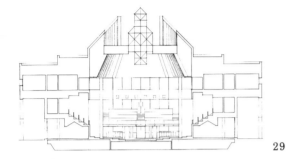

29

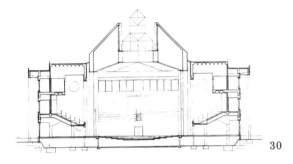

30

26 Model of Senate entry and offices
27 Model of Members' hall
28 Model of reception hall
29 Section through Senate chamber
30 Section through House chamber
31 Sketch of Members' hall
32 Model of House chamber
33 Model of Senate chamber

31

32

33

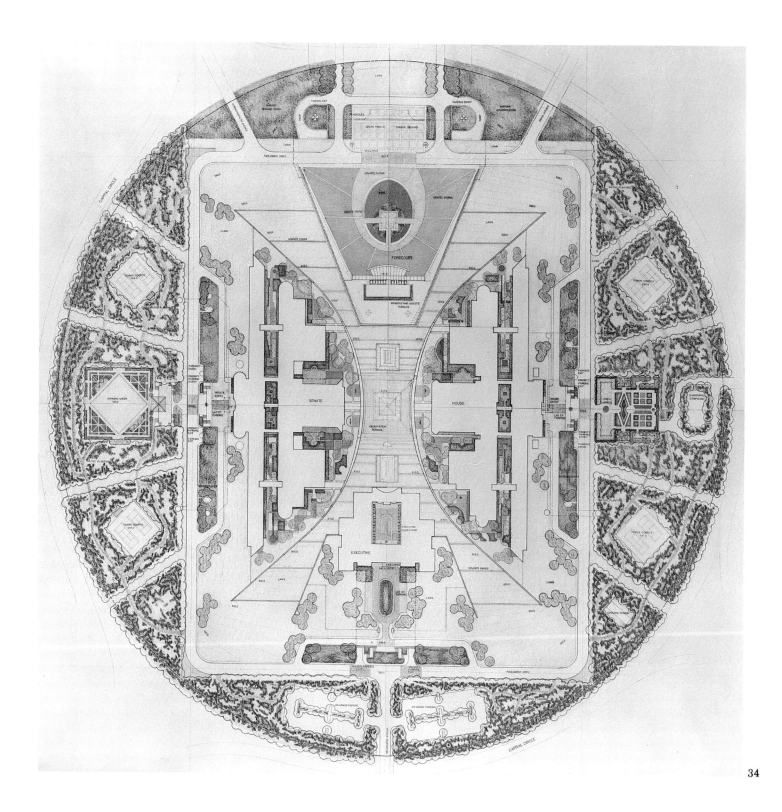

34 Site plan
35 Detail elevation of entry to the House chamber and offices

Parliament House Competition. Round 2

PHOTOGRAPHIC CREDITS

Alikakos, George, 66*(1)*
Bernard, Tom, 122*(2,3)*, 124*(10)*
Brett, James, 29*(1)*
Broches, Paul, 30*(5,6)*, 38*(7)*
Burri, Rene Magnum Photos, Inc., 26*(2,3)*, 27*(4-7)*, 28*(8)*
Checkman, Louis, 146*(6)*, 234*(6,8)*
Ciol, Elio, 192*(3)*, 193*(4-7)*, 194*(8-10)*, 195*(11)*, 196*(1-4)*, 197*(7,8)*, 198*(9-12)*, 199*(1,5,6)*, 200*(7-10)*, 201*(11)*
Cooper, Robert, 240*(15)*, 62*(18)*, 242*(22,23)*
Crane, Tom, 90*(6-8)*, 91*(10)*, 170*(1)*, 172*(6,7)*, 173*(8,9,11)*, 174*(13,14)*, 175*(15)*
Cserna, George, 140*(1)*, 141*(3-5)*, 142*(6-8)*, 143*(10)*, 61*(1)*
Georges, Alexandre, 21*(2)*, 116*(3,4)*
Giurgola, Adelaida, 155*(12-14)*
Giurgola, Romaldo, 20*(1)*, 21*(3)*
Guida, Harold, 48*(1,3)*, 50*(10)*, 82*(7,8)*, 83*(14)*, 166*(1,3)*, 167*(6)*, 173*(10)*, 174*(12)*, 217*(2)*, 218*(8)*
Kaufman, Elliott, 34*(8-10)*, 132*(15,17-20)*, 190*(7)*
Kurtz, John, 139*(10)*
La France, Rollin R., 22*(1)*, 23*(5-7)*, 24*(8,10-12)*, 25*(13)*, 32*(1)*, 33*(4)*, 34*(7)*, 44*(1)*, 46 *(5-7)*, 47*(8-10)*, 49*(7)*, 54*(1)*, 56*(6-8)*, 68*(1)*, 69*(4)*, 70*(6,7)*, 71*(9,10,12)*, 72*(1)*, 73*(4)*, 74 *(5-7)*, 75*(9,10)*, 76*(1,2)*, 78*(8,9)*, 79*(10,11)*, 80*(1)*, 88*(2,3)*, 89*(4)*, 90*(5)*, 91*(11)*, 92*(12-14)*, 93*(15)*, 112*(1)*, 113*(5,6)*, 114*(1)*, 116*(5)*, 117*(2,3)*, 118*(4)*, 119*(5)*, 120*(7)*, 121*(8,10-12)*, 123*(7)*, 127*(4)*, 129*(7-9)*, 130*(10)*, 131*(11-14)*, 132*(16)*, 136*(1)*, 138*(6-9)*, 139*(11,12)*, 156 *(4-6)*, 157*(7)*, 158*(8-10)*, 159*(11)*, 161*(3)*, 162*(4-7)*, 163*(9-11)*, 164*(12)*, 165*(13,14)*, 177 *(5)*, 178*(4)*, 180*(1)*, 181*(2)*, 182*(4-8)*, 185*(15-20)*, 186*(22,23)*, 187*(24)*, 188*(1)*, 190*(4-6)*, 191*(8,9)*, 206*(2,3)*, 209*(2)*, 210*(1,3,4)*, 216*(1)*, 217*(3-5)*, 218*(6,7)*, 219*(12)*, 221*(14-16)*, 222*(17-22)*, 223*(23)*, 225*(4-6)*, 229*(5)*
Lawson, John Q., 104*(1,4)*, 105*(5)*, 134*(4)*, 179*(5-8)*
Little, Rob, 236*(1)*
McGrath, Norman, 36*(1)*, 37*(5)*, 38*(6)*
Mitchell, Eric, 48*(4)*, 51*(11)*, 122*(1)*, 124*(9,11,12)*, 125*(13)*
Mitchell/Giurgola Architects, 52*(1)*, 53*(4-6)*, 55*(3)*, 61*(4)*, 81*(5)*, 103*(10)*, 106*(3)*, 153*(4)*, 206*(2,3)*
Namuth, Hans, 34*(6,11)*, 35*(12)*
Perry, G. Daniel, 56*(5,9)*, 57*(10)*, 59*(12)*
Pottle, John, 67*(2)*, 84*(1)*, 94*(1)*, 95*(6,7)*, 152*(1)*, 154*(9)*, 155*(10)*, 169*(5-7)*, 233*(2)*, 235 *(10)*
Rosenthal, Steve, 85*(4)*, 86*(8,9)*, 87*(10)*, 148*(2)*, 149*(4-6)*, 150*(8,9)*, 151*(11)*
Sadin, Abby, 82*(6,9-11)*, 83*(13)*
Sageser, Dart, 148*(1)*, 149*(7)*
Sandmeyer, Barbara, 48*(2,5)*
Sharp/Freeman, 226*(8)*, 227*(12)*
Spencer, Ken/Newsday, 39*(9)*
Sussman, Guy, 31*(8)*, 97*(5,6)*, 98*(9,10)*, 99*(11)*, 154*(7)*, 155*(11)*
Veltri, John, 166*(2)*, 167*(7)*, 184*(14)*, 186*(21)*
Wanner, Dick/Lancaster Newspapers, 50*(9)*
Yoshida, Michael, 133*(2)*, 134*(5)*, 135*(6,7)*

COLLABORATORS SINCE 1958

Partners

Ehrman B. Mitchell, Jr. FAIA
Romaldo Giurgola FAIA
Paul Broches AIA
Fred Foote FAIA
Steven M. Goldberg AIA
Harold S. Guida AIA, ARAIA*
Jan Keane AIA
Rollin R. LaFrance AIA
John Q. Lawson AIA
Richard G. Thorp ARAIA*

Associates

Michael Adams ARAIA*
Tim Halden Brown ARAIA*
Alan Greenberger AIA
John M. Kurtz AIA, ARAIA*
Randy Leach AIA
Lauren Mallas AIA
Mark J. Markiewicz AIA
John McNabb ARAIA*
Ann-Kathrin Olovson*
Dart Sageser AIA
Bruce Thompson AIA

* Mitchell/Giurgola & Thorp, Architects, Canberra, Australia

Employees

Edward Agoos, Giancarlo Alhadeff, Henry Altchek, Amy Anderson, Katherine Anderson, Marge Anderson, John Anhorn, Thomas Appelquist, Joel Baillere, Cliff Balch, Gordon Baldwin, Andrew Bank, Carl Barth, John Bauer, Charles Bauer, Pamela Beckerman, David Beem, Bernard Benn, Richard Bennett, Pamille Berg, Dennis Berg, Arthur Berg Jr, Ilona Berger, Phyllis Berman, John Blatteau, Sarah Boardman, Mario Boiardi, Francoise Bollack, Ralph Bolton, Nurith Bornstein, Debra Bowen, Clare Bracelin, James Braddock, Nancy Brandenburg, Michael Braun, Louise Braverman, Lynn Breslin, Carlos Brillembourg, Andrea Brown, Michael Brown, Richard Brown, James Bryan, Richmond Burton, Jack Cain, Anthony Calabretta, James Campbell, Lennox Caruth, Plato Chan, Edward Chapin, George Chapman, James Chapman, Peter Charapko, John Chase, In Joon Chung, Pietro Cicognani, Cathy Cinquina, Cathy Clymer, Bennett Colesberry Jr, James Comerford, Peter Coombs, Alexandra Coon, Ann Cozzubbo, Robert Crane III, Charles Dagit Jr, Joseph D'Ascenzo, Thomas Daley, Vishnukumar Dave, Alan Davies, Robert Davis Jr, Marlene Denzinger, Mark DeShong, Anthony Desnick, Frank DeVicaris, Barbara Diamantidis, Susan DiBona, Nicholas DiFilippo, Antonio Dimambro, Nancy Donovan, Joseph Druffel, Valerie Duhig, Steven Dumas, Harry Duncan, Jeremiah Eck, Dorothy Edwards, David Esch, William Fisher, Frank Fitzgibbons, Martin Fitzpatrick, Patricia Fletcher, Patrick Flory, Mary Fluke, David Ford, Oliver Ford, Lorraine Fox, William Fox, Robinson Fredenthal, Dale Furman, Victoria Garretson, Alfred Gilbert, Stephen Giles, Kathleen Gillen, Andre Gineste, John Godfrey Jr, Silvia Gmur, Michael Golubov, Michael Goodman, Douglas Gordon, Jan Gorlach, Stephen Gottlieb, Alexandru Grecu, William Gregg, Carolyn Grillo, Susan Grossman, Joyce Guerriero, Emmet Habgod Jr, Joyce Hager, Samuel Hanna III, Carolyn Haigh, Nori Hall, Frances Halsband, Tessa Jane Hancock, James Harb, Richard Harper, Brooke Harrington, Sally Harrison, John Hartley, Simone Hebert, Amy Hecht, Charles Held III, Curt Hemlepp, Hoyt Hilsman, James Hiser, Richard Hocking Jr, Lali Holmes, Maureen Hotz, Sharon Howell, Ronald Huff, Lisa Interollo, Franklin Israel, Jacqueline Jacullo, Valerie Jaudon, Everardo Jefferson, William Jennings, Patricia Johanson, Stephen Johnson, Gregg Jones, Leon Jurski, Carol Karasek, Ada Karmi, Charles Kattman, Lorna Katz, Margaret Keleshiam, Emmanuel Kelley, Daniel Kelley, Lawrence Kenny, Betty King, John Kirwan, Robert Kitchen, Robert Kliment, Michael Kline, Gladys Knight, Douglas Kochel, Scott Koniecko, Kenneth Kornstein, James Kruhly, Karl Krumholtz, Suzanne Labarthe, Sinikka Laine, Michael Landau, Christopher Landis, Harry Langhorne Jr, Richard LaSerre, Brooke Laughlin, Eric Lautzenheiser, Rolando Laveist, Duc Won Lee, Wai-Nung Lee, Joseph Lengeling, Joyce Lenhardt, Karen Lennox, Lotus Leong, Stephen Levine, Carol Levy, John Lewis, Gerald Li, Joan Lind, Donna Lisle, Jay Litman, Donna Litostansky, Stephanie Liva, Laura Locicero, Thelma Lockhard, Carol Loewenson, Samuel Logan III, Thomas Lonnecker, Tiffany Lowrey, Victoria Lucas, Thomas Lurcott, Barbara Macaulay, Zsuzsa MacDonald, Robert MacIntyre, Theodore Maggos, Vincent Maiello, Norman Malin, Michael Manfredi, Caren Marks, Judy Mattingly, Joseph McCarthy, John McCoy, Kirby Mehrhof, Jaimini Mehta, Benjamin Mendelsund, Spass Merdjanoff, Sigrid Miller, Eric Mitchell, Angela Monferrato, Sharon Moore, Donleroy Morales, Nelson Munoz, Hilda Murphy, Solomon Myzel, Susan Nace, Robert Nalls, Deborah Natsios, Margaret Nave, Sallie Naylor, William Newbold Jr, Renee Newstein, William Odum, Suzanne O'Keefe, Nanayo Onose, John Orfield, Jesse Ozarowski, Jon Paddock, Peter Parsons, Nora Peck, Philip Pente Jr, Daniel Perry, Cecil Peterson, David Peterson, Peter Petrall, Scott Phillips, John Pihl, Robert Pils, Patricia Pitcher, Carlous Pitts, Patrick Plottier, Ingo Pop, Ulrich Poulsen, Charlette Present, Francis Prevose, Lansing Pugh, Werner Rafflenbeul, Christopher Raker, John Randolph, Eliza Reilly, Robin Reshetar, James Rich, Owen Richards, Reginald Richey, Joan Roberts, Donna Robertson, Barbara Robinson, Bonita Roche, Nadine Rollins, John Romano, Ronnie Rosenblatt, Marvin Rosenman, Luigi Rosselli, Michael Rubenstein, Ronald Sable, Barbara Sageser, Franklin Salasky, Leonard Salvato, Peter Saylor, Lynn Schneider, William Schweber, Jacqueline Scott, Elsbeth Selver, Margie Shoenewald, Robert Shuman, Leonard Siegel, Jabir Sikka, James Simon, Karsten Simonsen, Clifford Slavin, Floris Smith, Charlene Smith, Gil Snyder, Maureen Sorrells, Michael Spatz, Gloria Stallfort, Susan Stando, Max Steele, Nancy Steele, Christopher Stein, Jack Stevens, Dale Strachan, Joyce Streibig, John Stroik, Elko Stuiver, David Stupplebean, Ross Styles, Douglas Suisman, Michael Sullivan, Collene Thomas, James Thomas, Marianna Thomas, Douglas Thompson, Mark Thompson, Robert Thrun, Robert Tobin, Mary Train, Rosanna Trasatti, Nancy Twitchell, Noel Tyson, Carolyn Uhl, Carlos Enrique Vallhonrat, Willy VanBel, David Vaughan, Leslie Ventsch, Alexei Vergun, Marvin Verman, Louis Villa, Roy Vollmer, John Vosmek, Herman Wai, Usman Wal, John Walker, Lawrence Walsh, Carl Walter III, Clarence Wang, Sheldon Weber, Fran Webster, Mark Werther, John West, Bernard Wharton, Cindy White, Denyce Williams, Christopher Williamson, Daniell Wills, Pamela Terry Wilson, Wulff Winkelvoss, Deborah Wolinsky, Mary Woodward, Nancy Woogmaster, James Wright Jr, Stanford Wyatt Jr, Walter Wycoff, Robert York, Michael Yoshida, Lanie Young, George Yu, William Zdravkovic, Benuel Zook.

CHRONOLOGY OF PROJECTS

1958 CROCKETT RESIDENCE
Corning, New York

EXHIBITION DESIGN
Far East Asia Development Project
New York Coliseum, New York
With Wright and Mitarachi

MITCHELL RESIDENCE
Lafayette Hill, Pennsylvania

PHILADELPHIA CHAPTER CENTENNIAL, EXHIBITION DESIGN
American Institute of Architects
Philadelphia, Pennsylvania

1959 HOME DESIGN SHOW, EXHIBITION DESIGN
Brooklyn Museum
Brooklyn, New York
With Kallman and Mitarachi

OFFICES AND WAREHOUSE
Kurtz Brothers, Eastern Division
Valley Forge, Pennsylvania

PUBLIC HEALTH CENTER NO. 9
City of Philadelphia
Philadelphia, Pennsylvania

STINE RESIDENCE
Bryan, Ohio

1960 EASTERN EXPRESS TERMINAL
Philadelphia, Pennsylvania
With Miller-Vrydagh-Miller

EVANSVILLE PETROLEUM CLUB, INTERIORS
Evansville Petroleum Club
Evansville, Indiana

*WRIGHT BROTHERS MEMORIAL VISITOR CENTER
National Park Service
Kill Devil Hills, North Carolina

1961 FRANKLIN DELANO ROOSEVELT MEMORIAL, COMPETITION
Franklin Delano Roosevelt Memorial
Washington, D.C.
Honorable Mention

*HUEBNER HALL
The American College
Bryn Mawr, Pennsylvania

MEDNICK RESIDENCE
Philadelphia, Pennsylvania

NATIONAL CONVENTION FINE ARTS, EXHIBITION DESIGN
American Institute of Architects
Philadelphia, Pennsylvania

TOWN HOUSE DEVELOPMENT
Lumberyard Development Corporation
Philadelphia, Pennsylvania
Project

1962 BOSTON CITY HALL, COMPETITION
City of Boston
Boston, Massachusetts
One of eight finalists

CAMPUS PLAN
Academy of the New Church (ANC)
Bryn Athyn, Pennsylvania

HOUSING 7901 HENRY AVENUE
Philadelphia, Pennsylvania
Project

*MARKET STREET EAST DEVELOPMENT PLAN
Philadelphia City Planning Commission
Philadelphia, Pennsylvania

*OFFICE BUILDING ADDITION
Philadelphia Life Insurance Company
Philadelphia, Pennsylvania

STUDENT DORMITORY
Academy of the New Church
Bryn Athyn, Pennsylvania

1963 *ADMINISTRATION BUILDING
Academy of the New Church
Bryn Athyn, Pennsylvania

ANDALE COMPANY OFFICE BUILDING
18th and Cherry Corporation
Lansdale, Pennsylvania

FRANKFORD ARSENAL METROLOGY LABORATORIES
United States Army Corps of Engineers
Philadelphia, Pennsylvania

LABORATORY AND CLASSROOM RENOVATION
University of Pennsylvania
Philadelphia, Pennsylvania

LAWRENCE COURT DEVELOPMENT
Philadelphia, Pennsylvania
Project with Clifford B. Slavin

MAINTENANCE BUILDING
Academy of the New Church
Bryn Athyn, Pennsylvania
Project

PATZAU RESIDENCE
Philadelphia, Pennsylvania
Project

*Asterisks denote projects included in the book

TEL AVIV REDEVELOPMENT PLAN, COMPETITION
City of Tel Aviv
Tel Aviv, Israel
Submission

WALNUT STREET PARKING GARAGE
University of Pennsylvania
Philadelphia, Pennsylvania

WHITE RESIDENCE
Chestnut Hill, Pennsylvania

1964 OFFICE BUILDING
Bethlehem Steel
Philadelphia, Pennsylvania
Project

1965 ACADIA NATIONAL PARK HEADQUARTERS BUILDING
National Park Service
Bar Harbor, Maine
Project

CHURCH AND SCHOOL FACILITIES
Swarthmore Presbyterian Church
Swarthmore, Pennsylvania
Project

INTERNATIONAL HOUSE, COMPETITION
International House
Philadelphia, Pennsylvania
Submission

NATIONAL HEADQUARTERS BUILDING, COMPETITION
American Institute of Architects
Washington, D.C.
Winning submission 1965/Project 1967/Project 1978

NEWMAN CENTER
University of Kentucky
Lexington, Kentucky
Project

*MYRICK PAVILION
The American College
Bryn Mawr, Pennsylvania

1966 BOSTON 5 CENT SAVINGS BANK COMPETITION
Boston 5 Cent Savings Bank
Boston, Massachusetts
Submission

*CAMPUS PLAN
The American College
Bryn Mawr, Pennsylvania,

PERKINS RESIDENCE
Philadelphia, Pennsylvania
With Roy Vollmer

1967 CENTRAL BUSINESS DISTRICT PLAN
City of Wilkes Barre
Wilkes Barre, Pennsylvania

HOTEL AND OFFICE BUILDING
Wilmington Corporation
Wilmington, Delaware
Project

PARKING GARAGE
New York State University Construction Fund
Oneonta, New York
Project

WILLIAM JEANES MEMORIAL LIBRARY
Whitemarsh Township
Whitemarsh, Pennsylvania
Project

1968 INTERIM FACILITIES
United Nations International School
New York, New York

INTERNATIONAL EXPOSITION
14th Triennale di Milano
Milan, Italy
With Lyndon and Shapira

ROBERTS RESIDENCE
Philadelphia, Pennsylvania

THEATER FOR ROCKEFELLER CENTER
Robert Whitehead
New York, New York
Project

UNITED STATES EMBASSY, BOGOTA
United States Department of State
Bogota, Columbia
Project

ZEBOOKER RESIDENCE
Philadelphia, Pennsylvania

1969 PERMANENT FACILITIES
United Nations International School
New York, New York
Feasibility Study

1970 *CAMPUS PLAN UPDATING
Swarthmore College
Swarthmore, Pennsylvania 1970-1978

*DAYTON RESIDENCE
Wayzata, Minnesota

MUSEUM PARKING GARAGE
University of Pennsylvania
Philadelphia, Pennsylvania

*30th STREET SITE MASTER PLAN
The Philadelphia 1976 Bicentennial Corporation
Philadelphia, Pennsylvania
With David A. Crane

WOMEN'S PHYSICAL EDUCATION FACILITY
Swarthmore College
Swarthmore, Pennsylvania
Project

1971 ROOSEVELT RESIDENTIAL DEVELOPMENT
New York State Urban Development Corporation
Roosevelt Island, New York
Project

*SOUTH END BRANCH PUBLIC LIBRARY
City of Boston
Boston, Massachusetts

*SUBWAY CONCOURSE ENTRANCE
City of Philadelphia
Philadelphia, Pennsylvania

*UNITED WAY HEADQUARTERS BUILDING
United Way of Southeastern Pennsylvania
Philadelphia, Pennsylvania

*UNIVERSITY MUSEUM ACADEMIC WING
University of Pennsylvania
Philadelphia, Pennsylvania

1972 BOK TOWER
American Foundation
Lake Wales, Florida

CENTER FOR TRANSFER OF INFORMATION
University City Science Center
Philadelphia, Pennsylvania
Feasibility Study

CONVENTION CENTER MASTER PLAN
University City Science Center
Philadelphia, Pennsylvania
Project

*EASTWICK SITE MASTER PLAN
The Philadelphia 1976 Bicentennial Corporation
Philadelphia, Pennsylvania
With the offices of Louis I. Kahn; Venturi
and Rauch; Bower and Fradley; Murphy, Levy,
Wurman; Eshbach, Glass, Kale & Associates

*MDRT FOUNDATION HALL
The American College
Bryn Mawr, Pennsylvania

*MISSION PARK RESIDENTIAL HOUSES
Williams College
Williamstown, Massachusetts

PEACOCK HILL REDEVELOPMENT PLAN
Colonial Williamsburg Foundation
Williamsburg, Virginia

TWIN PARKS EAST HOUSING DEVELOPMENT
New York City Housing Development
The Bronx, New York
Project

1973 ADMINISTRATIVE OFFICE INTERIORS, G BUILDING
Westinghouse Electric Corporation
Lester, Pennsylvania

ADMINISTRATIVE OFFICE INTERIORS, N BUILDING
Westinghouse Electric Corporation
Lester, Pennsylvania

CENTRAL SERVICE BUILDING
Westinghouse Electric Corporation
Lester, Pennsylvania

*COLUMBUS EAST HIGH SCHOOL
Bartholomew Consolidated School Corporation
Columbus, Indiana

*CORRECTIONAL FACILITIES STUDY
American Foundation
Publication

*EUGENE M. AND THERESA LANG MUSIC BUILDING
Swarthmore College
Swarthmore, Pennsylvania

PHYSICAL EDUCATION FACILITIES
Swarthmore College
Swarthmore, Pennsylvania
Feasibility study

UNIVERSITY MUSEUM, EXHIBITIONS
University of Pennsylvania
Philadelphia, Pennsylvania

UNIVERSITY MUSEUM, RENOVATION AND EXHIBITION PLANNING
University of Pennsylvania
Philadelphia, Pennsylvania
Project

*WORSHIP ASSEMBLY
Benedictine Society of St. Bede
Peru, Illinois

1974 CASA THOMAS JEFFERSON
United States Information Agency/
Thomas Jefferson Cultural Council
Brasilia, D.F., Brazil

SPRINGHOUSE RESEARCH CENTER, MASTER PLAN
Rohm and Haas Corporation
Springhouse, Pennsylvania
Project

*STUDENT UNION, STATE UNIVERSITY COLLEGE AT PLATTSBURGH
New York State University Construction Fund
Plattsburgh, New York

WAINWRIGHT STATE OFFICE COMPLEX, COMPETITION
State of Missouri
St. Louis, Missouri
Winning submission, with Hastings & Chivetta Architects, Planners

1975 BICENTENNIAL EXHIBIT
Philadelphia-Baltimore-Washington Stock Exchange, Inc.
Philadelphia, Pennsylvania
Project

*CONDON HALL, SCHOOL OF LAW
University of Washington
Seattle, Washington

EXHIBITION
Peale House, Pennsylvania Academy of the Fine Arts
Philadelphia, Pennsylvania

FRANKLIN SQUARE STATION
Delaware River Port Authority
Philadelphia, Pennsylvania
Feasibility study

GRIFFIN MEMORIAL, COMPETITION
City of Canberra, Australia

*INDIAN POINT ENERGY EDUCATION CENTER
Consolidated Edison Company of New York, Inc.
Buchanan, New York

*LIBERTY BELL PAVILION
National Park Service
Philadelphia, Pennsylvania

OFFICE INTERIORS
University City Science Center
Philadelphia, Pennsylvania

*PENN MUTUAL TOWER, CORPORATE HEADQUARTERS
Penn Mutual Life Insurance Company
Philadelphia, Pennsylvania

SCHOOL RENOVATION AND ADDITION
St. Peter's School
Philadelphia, Pennsylvania
Project

*TWO INA PLAZA, OFFICE BUILDING
Insurance Company of North America
Philadelphia, Pennsylvania

UNDERGRADUATE HOUSING
Yale University
New Haven, Connecticut
Project

VISITORS CENTER AND OBSERVATION DECK, EXHIBITION
Penn Mutual Life Insurance Company
Philadelphia, Pennsylvania

WALT WHITMAN INTERNATIONAL CENTER FOR POETRY
City of Camden
Camden, New Jersey
Project

*WILLIAM PENN HIGH SCHOOL
City of Philadelphia Board of Education
Philadelphia, Pennsylvania

1976 *OFFICE AND ASSEMBLY BUILDING
U.S. Car Manufacturing Division
Volvo of America Corporation
Chesapeake, Virginia

LIVING HISTORY CENTER/PHILADELPHIA BICENTENNIAL
City of Philadelphia
Philadelphia, Pennsylvania

MAIN OFFICE RENOVATION
Girard Bank
Philadelphia, Pennsylvania

MEDICAL CLINIC
Clymer Clinic
Quakertown, Pennsylvania
Feasibility study

POWER HOUSE
Volvo of America Corporation
Chesapeake, Virginia

SENIOR CITIZEN'S HOUSING, COMPETITION
St. Joseph's Village
Brookhaven, New York

*TREDYFFRIN PUBLIC LIBRARY
Tredyffrin Township
Strafford, Pennsylvania

1977 *BENJAMIN F. FEINBERG LIBRARY, STATE UNIVERSITY COLLEGE AT PLATTSBURGH
New York State University Construction Fund
Plattsburgh, New York

FRANKLIN DELANO ROOSEVELT MEMORIAL
New York State Urban Development Corporation
New York, New York
Project, with David Wisdom Associates

HARBOR PLAZA MASTER PLAN, OFFICE/PARKING/HOTEL COMPLEX
Collins Development Corporation
Stamford, Connecticut

MAIN ENTRANCE COURT
The Salk Institute
La Jolla, California
Project

OFFICE BUILDING, COMPETITION
Texas Commerce Bank
Houston, Texas
Submission

*SHERMAN FAIRCHILD CENTER FOR THE LIFE SCIENCES
Columbia University
New York, New York

*UNITED STATES CAPITOL MASTER PLAN FOR THE FUTURE
DEVELOPMENT OF THE CAPITOL GROUNDS AND RELATED AREAS
Architect of the Capitol
Washington, D.C. 1977-81
Design consultant with Wallace, Roberts & Todd

*WESTLAKE PARK, HOTEL/RETAIL/PARKING COMPLEX
Mondev International Limited
Seattle, Washington
Project with Joyce Copeland Vaughn and Nordfors

1978 DE CORDOVA MUSEUM
Renovation/Addition Master Plan
De Cordova Museum
Lincoln, Massachusetts
Project

*EAST CAMPUS DEVELOPMENT PLAN
Massachusetts Institute of Technology
Cambridge, Massachusetts
With Gruzen & Partners

NURSING HOME
Mr. Hardie A. Beloff
West Goshen, Pennsylvania
Project

ORAL HYGIENE CENTER, SCHOOL OF DENTAL MEDICINE
University of Pennsylvania
Philadelphia, Pennsylvania
Project

RENOVATION AND ADDITION
Philadelphia College of Art
Philadelphia, Pennsylvania
Project

RESIDENCE KITCHEN ADDITION
Philadelphia, Pennsylvania

RETREAT HOUSE IN NORTHERN EUROPE
Project

*ROMA INTERROTTA EXHIBITION
Incontri Internazionali d'Arte
Rome, Italy

1979 *ADMINISTRATIVE RESOURCES CENTER
Lukens Steel Company
Coatesville, Pennsylvania

THE ART MUSEUM, MASTER PLAN
Princeton University
Princeton, New Jersey

*BENI STABILI APARTMENT/RETAIL COMPLEX
Beni Stabili U.S.A., Inc.
Houston, Texas

CENTRAL CHILLED WATER PLANT, MASSACHUSETTS
INSTITUTE OF TECHNOLOGY
Syska & Hennessy Engineers
Cambridge, Massachusetts
Project, with Gruzen & Partners

GENERAL SERVICES BUILDING
The American College
Bryn Mawr, Pennsylvania

*KASPERSON RESIDENCE
Conestoga, Pennsylvania

*NEWMAN RESIDENCE
Bedford, New York

OFFICE INTERIORS
Blank, Rome, Comisky & McCauley
Philadelphia, Pennsylvania

*PHYSICAL ACTIVITIES BUILDING
Swarthmore College
Swarthmore, Pennsylvania

REGIONAL HEADQUARTERS, COMPETITION
South Central Bell Telephone Company
Nashville, Tennessee
Submission, with Gassner, Nathan & Partners

*STRAWBERRY SQUARE, OFFICE BUILDING/RETAIL/PARKING
Harristown Development Corporation
Harrisburg, Pennsylvania
With Lawrie and Green, Architects

*TEN STAMFORD FORUM, OFFICE BUILDING/PARKING GARAGE
F.D. Rich Company
Stamford New Urban Corporation Subsidiary
Stamford, Connecticut

1980 *BOOKSTORE & LOUNGE
Union Theological Seminary
New York, New York

CELL BIOLOGY RESEARCH CENTER, RENOVATION
New York University
New York, New York
Project

*GEOLOGY LIBRARY, RENOVATION AND ADDITION
Princeton University
Princeton, New Jersey

MEN'S SHELTER FEASIBILITY STUDY
The Vera Institute
New York, New York

*WESTLAKE PARK, MUSEUM/RETAIL/PARKING COMPLEX
Mondev International Limited
Seattle, Washington
Project

1981 BATTERY PARK CITY, COMMERCIAL CENTER,
DEVELOPMENT COMPETITION
Olympia and York Equity Corporation
New York, New York

*COLLEGE OF HEALTH SCIENCES, TECHNOLOGY AND
MANAGEMENT BUILDING
Massachusetts Institute of Technology
Cambridge, Massachusetts
With Gruzen & Partners

*CONCERT THEATER, RENOVATION AND RECONSTRUCTION
C.W. Post Center, Long Island University
Greenvale, New York

*ELEMENTARY SCHOOL
Associazione Nazionale Alpini/
U.S. Agency for International Development
Aviano, Italy

GENERAL OFFICE BUILDING
State of Washington
Olympia, Washington
Project, with Joyce/Nordfors and Associates

*GRADUATE CENTER
The American College
Bryn Mawr, Pennsylvania

*HEALTH SERVICES BUILDING
Massachusetts Institute of Technology
Cambridge, Massachusetts
With Gruzen & Partners

LINCOLN WEST, HOTEL/APARTMENT COMPLEX
Lincoln West Associates
New York, New York
Project

*MAINTENANCE FACILITY, INDEPENDENCE PARK
National Park Service
Philadelphia, Pennsylvania

*STUDENT HOUSING
Associazione Nazionale Alpini/
U.S. Agency for International Development
San Pietro al Natisone, Italy

TECHNICAL HIGH SCHOOL
Associazione Nazionale Alpini/
U.S. Agency for International Development
Maniago, Italy

*WAINWRIGHT STATE OFFICE COMPLEX
State of Missouri
St. Louis, Missouri
With Hastings and Chivetta, Architects, Planners

*WESTLAKE PARK, MUSEUM/RETAIL/PARKING COMPLEX
Daon Pacific, Inc.
Seattle, Washington
Project, with Joyce/Nordfors and Associates

WUNSCH ARTS CENTER, RENOVATION
Council on the Arts at Glen Cove
Glen Cove, New York

1982 *KNOLL INTERNATIONAL MANUFACTURING FACILITY, MASTER
PLAN
Knoll International
East Greenville, Pennsylvania

LOS PALOS GRANDES, OFFICE BUILDING/RETAIL COMPLEX
Nicholas Simon, Developer
Caracas, Venezuela
With W. James Alcock, Architect

WALTER ROYAL DAVIS LIBRARY
THE UNIVERSITY OF NORTH CAROLINA AT CHAPEL HILL
Chapel Hill, North Carolina
With Leslie N. Boney, Architect

STUDENT CENTER
Bryn Mawr College
Bryn Mawr, Pennsylvania 1982

1983 *LIBRARY RENOVATION
Union Theological Seminary
New York, New York

*SCHECHTER GROUP BUILDING
The Schechter Group
New York, New York

Future Completion

*LAFAYETTE PLACE, HOTEL/RETAIL/COMPLEX
Lafayette Place Associates
Boston, Massachusetts 1983

*NATIONAL PLACE, HOTEL/OFFICE/RETAIL/PARKING COMPLEX
Square 254 Limited Partnership
Washington, D.C. 1983
With Frank Schlesinger FAIA, Architect/Planners

ANCHORAGE HISTORICAL AND FINE ARTS MUSEUM
Municipality of Anchorage
Anchorage, Alaska 1984
With Maynard & Partch

ANNENBERG SCHOOL OF COMMUNICATIONS, ADDITION AND
RENOVATION
University of Pennsylvania
Philadelphia, Pennsylvania 1984

*THE ART MUSEUM, RENOVATION AND ADDITION
Princeton University
Princeton, New Jersey 1984

*ASSEMBLY/SHIPPING FACILITY, PHASE I
Knoll International
East Greenville, Pennsylvania 1984

*COLUMBIA AVENUE STATION IMPROVEMENTS
City of Philadelphia and Temple University
Philadelphia, Pennsylvania 1984

*CORPORATE HEADQUARTERS BUILDING
AB Volvo Holding Company
Gothenburg, Sweden 1984

GALLERIA HOTEL
Carrozzo Properties Ltd.
Oklahoma City, Oklahoma 1984

KERSHAW RESIDENCE
Montgomery, Alabama 1984

UNITED STATES EMBASSY, JAMAICA
United States Department of State
Kingston, Jamaica 1984

*WILSHIRE-GLENDON OFFICE BUILDING
Wilshire-Glendon Associates, Ltd.
Los Angeles, California 1985
With Daniel, Mann, Johnson & Mendenhall

*PARLIAMENT HOUSE AUSTRALIA
Parliament House Construction Authority
Canberra, Australia 1988
Mitchell/Giurgola & Thorp Architects

BIBLIOGRAPHY

"Two Visitors' Centers Exemplify New Park Architecture," *Progressive Architecture,* February 1959, p. 87.

"Mitchell & Giurgola Replan a Rittenhouse Square Penthouse for a Family of Music and Art Lovers," *Interiors,* August 1959, pp. 82-83.

Scully, Vincent, Jr., "New Talent U.S.A.," *Art in America,* January 1961, p. 67.

Burchard, John Ely, "Debating the FDR Memorial: A Plea for Relevance," *Architectural Record,* March 1961, pp. 177-182.

"New Town Houses for Center City," *Downtown,* March 31-April 7, 1961, pp. 1-2.

Rowan, Jan C., "Wanting to Be. The Philadelphia School," *Progressive Architecture,* April 1961, pp. 131-155.

Reece, Ilse Meissner, "Possibilities for Individual Choice: Thoughts on Urban Housing," *Progressive Architecture,* October 1961, pp. 124-127.

Rowan, Jan C., "Offices Near Philadelphia," *Progressive Architecture,* December 1961, pp. 122-131.

Van Trump, James D., "Pilgrimage to the Present," *Charrette,* April 1962, pp. 8-12.

American Federation of Arts, *1962 National Gold Medal Exhibition of the Building Arts,* Architectural League of New York, New York, April 1962, p. 55.

"Ten Americans To Watch," *Pagent,* February 1963, pp. 55-56.

Collins, Peter, "Runner Up in the Boston City Hall Competition," *Progressive Architecture,* April 1963, pp. 149-153.

"Remodeled Stable by Aldo Giurgola," *Interiors,* May 1963, pp. 120-121.

Rowan, Jan C., "Kitty Hawk Museum," *Progressive Architecture,* August 1963, pp. 112-120.

Lyndon, Donlyn, "Filologia dell'Architettura Americana," *Casabella,* November 1963, pp. 8-40.

Von Eckardt, Wolf, "The Park Service Dares to Build Well," *The Washington Post,* 29 March 1964, Section G, p. G6.

Lutz, Mark, "Living in Chestnut Hill," *Chestnut Hill Local,* 15 July 1964, p. 2.

"University Parking Garage," *Progressive Architecture,* December 1964, pp. 146-151.

"AIA Headquarters Building Competition," *AIA Journal,* January 1965, pp. 23-26.

"Mitchell et Giurgola Parking Garage de l'Université de Pennsylvanie," *L'Architecture D'Aujourd'hui,* March 1965, pp. 46-47.

"Six Philadelphia Architects," *Arts and Architecture,* April 1965, pp. 16-23.

"Conscious Contrasts," *Progressive Architecture,* May 1965, pp. 137-141.

"Buildings in the News. Bower and Fradley Win International House Competition in Philadelphia," *Architectural Record,* October 1965, p. 41.

Vreeland, Thomas R. Jr., "Project for Tel Aviv-Yaffo Town Planning Competition," *Arts and Architecture,* January 1966, pp. 28-31.

McQuade, Walter (ed.), "Structure and Design. Companies With A Designing Eye," *Fortune,* March 1966, pp. 161-162.

Pile, J., *Drawings of Architectural Interiors,* Whitney Library of Design, New York, 1967.

"Young American Architects," *Zodiac* 17, 1967, pp. 127-135.

"Revised Plan for AIA Headquarters Spurned by Fine Arts Commission," *Progressive Architecture,* July 1967, p. 48.

"AIA Headquarters: Headquarters for Architecture," *Progressive Architecture,* December 1967, pp. 136-140.

"Remodeling: How to Salvage Unlivable Space," *House and Garden,* May 1968, pp. 90-91.

Scully, Vincent, Jr., *American Architecture and Urbanism,* Frederick A. Praeger, New York, 1969.

Stern, Robert A. M., *New Directions in American Architecture,* George Braziller, New York, 1969.

D'Antona, B., "The Reinforced Concrete Influence in the Contemporaneous North-American Architecture," *L'Industria Italiana del Cemento,* January 1969, pp. 17-52.

Gueft, Olga, "Protean Student Union as the Urban Core for an Academic Community," *Interiors,* November 1969, pp. 120-130.

Warburton, Ralph, "Design for Individuality," *HUD Challenge,* November-December 1969, pp. 26-28.

Smith, C. Ray, "The Great Museum Debate," *Progressive Architecture,* December 1969, pp. 76-85.

Aloi, Roberto, *50 Ville Del Nostro Tempo,* Ulrico Hoepli Editore, Milan, 1970.

"Citation. Williams College Residential Houses," *Progressive Architecture,* January 1970, pp. 94-95.

"One Man's Will," *Architectural Design,* August 1970, p. 375.

Gueft, Olga (ed.), "Romaldo Giurgola," *Interiors,* November 1970, pp. 126-131.

Jacoby, Helmut, *New Techniques of Architectural Rendering,* Frederick A. Praeger, New York, 1971.

"How 1970 Award-Winning Schools Compare," *Nation's Schools,* January 1971, pp. 41-59.

Dixon, John Morris, "Philadelphia. Small United Fund office building plays an important role in the urban scene," *Architectural Forum,* January 1971, pp. 40-45.

Koehler, Robert E., "Our Park Service Serves Architecture Well," *AIA Journal,* January 1971, pp. 18-25.

Museums Association of India, *Museum Architecture. Proceedings of the All India Museums Conference,* New Delhi: n.p., 1-4 February 1971.

"Tower truss will link core to composition wall," *Engineering News-Record,* 18 March 1971, pp. 60-61.

"Mitchell/Giurgola design flexible high school," *American School & University,* July 1971, pp. 21-22.

"Selearchitettura," *L'Architettura,* August 1971, pp. 250-251.

"Buildings that save a watt, and more," *Progressive Architecture,* October 1971, pp. 104-111.

Donohue, Victoria, "University Museum: New Wing, New Era," *The Philadelphia Inquirer,* 24 October 1971, Section H, p. 3.

"Headquarters Building, United Fund of the Philadelphia Area, Philadelphia, Pa.," *Werk,* January 1972, pp. 32-33.

"Works of Mitchell-Giurgola," *Space Design,* Special Issue, February 1972, pp. 5-84.

"Giurgola's Craft," *Architectural Review,* March 1972, p. 189.

Marlin, William, "Excavating the Present. A Museum of Anthropology Builds its Missing Link," *Architectural Forum,* March 1972, pp. 40-45.

Gabetti, Roberto, A. Isola, G. Ranieri, L. Re, T. Vernetti, "Contesto Urbano e Coerenza in Architettura," *Moebius 3,* June 1972, pp. 27-33.

Di Nardo, Giorgio and Gianni Siciliano, "La Citta nell'Edificio. Lo Studio Giurgola-Mitchell di Filadelfia," *Moebius 3,* June 1972, pp. 64-73.

Zevi, Bruno, "Il Rinascimento ha Messo la Coda," *L'Espresso,* 20 August 1972, p. 20.

Marlin, William, "Everyday Buildings. The Boston Public Facilities Department gives esthetics and economy equal time," *Architectural Forum,* October 1972, pp. 40-49.

Jensen, Robert, "Mitchell/Giurgola Associates: Three Projects," *Architectural Record,* October 1972, pp.105-114.

"United Fund Building, Philadelphia, Pa., U.S.A.," *Cembureau Photonews,* 2 November 1972, p. 8.

"Bauspeigel. Subway. Museum," *Arkitektur Aktuell* 32, November 1972, pp. 54-55.

Zadra, Federico, "Il nuovo garage dell' Universita di Pennsylvania a Filadelfia," *L'Industria Italiana del Cemento,* November 1972, pp. 743-806.

"A Residence in Minnesota," *Domus* 517, December 1972, pp. 12-19.

Kemper, A. M., *Drawings by American Architects,* John Wiley & Sons, New York, 1973.

Veltri, J., *Photographing Architecture,* Amphoto, New York, 1973.

Zevi, Bruno, *Spaci dell'Architettura Moderna,* Einaudi, Turin, 1973.

Morton, David A., "Complimenting the Past," *Progressive Architecture,* February 1973, pp. 56-61.

"Columbus High School, Columbus, Ind.," *L'Architecture D'Aujourd'hui,* March 1973, pp. 63-65.

"New Havens at Yale," *Architectural Forum,* March 1973, p. 20.

"Works of Mitchell/Giurgola. Practice for the Concept of the City Through Architecture," *Space Design,* April 1973, pp. 33-78.

"American College of Life Underwriters MDRT Foundation Hall," *Architecture + Urbanism,* April 1973, pp. 37-48.

"News Plus. Mr. Blandings Builds His Dream Headquarters," *Architecture Plus,* May 1973, p. 86.

"AIA/HQ," *Architectural Record,* May 1973, pp. 131-139.

Kazuhiro, Ishii, "Notes Concerning the Open School—as a Children's Community," *Space Design,* June 1973, pp. 83-98.

"Focus. Foreign Intrigue," *Architectural Forum,* June 1973, p. 10.

"Mitchell/Giurgola," *Architecture + Urbanism,* June 1973, pp. 69-92.

"News Plus. Best Mole Hole," *Architecture Plus,* July 1973, p. 16.

Marlin, William, "What do architects build for themselves?" *Christian Science Monitor,* 20 July 1973, p. 12.

Von Eckardt, Wolf, "An Oasis of Humanism," *The Washington Post,* 21 July 1973, pp. 81, 83.

Brandston, Howard, "A Profession Grows Up," *Progressive Architecture,* September 1973, pp. 74-78.

"Mitchell/Giurgola: la MDRT Foundation Hall," *L'Industria delle Construzioni* 37, September-October 1973, pp. 94-99.

"Mitchell/Giurgola Show," *Art Alliance Bulletin,* October 1973, p. 11.

Stephens, Suzanne, "Magnificent Intentions," *Architectural Forum,* October 1973, pp. 36-43.

"Focus. One for All," *Architectural Forum,* November 1973, pp. 12-13.

Brick & Tile, Brick Institute of America, McLean, Va., November/December 1973.

Goldberger, Paul, "Energy Crisis May Doom Era of Glass Towers," *The New York Times,* 6 December 1973, pp. 49, 93.

Katz, Jamie, "New Life for the Life Sciences," *Columbia College Today,* Winter 1973-1974, pp. 4-9.

"Residence, Wayzata, Minnesota," *Architecture + Urbanism,* March 1974, pp. 19-26.

"News Report. Buildings on the Way Up," *Progressive Architecture,* March 1974, pp. 20-21.

"Focus. In Context at Columbia," *Architectural Forum,* March 1974, p. 8.

Huxtable, Ada Louise, "Of Capital Failure and Capital Crime," *The New York Times,* 17 March 1974, Section II, p. 27.

"AIA Announces Winners of 1974 Honor Awards," *F.W. Dodge Construction News,* 26 April 1974, pp. 24-26.

"MDRT Foundation Hall, Bryn Mawr, Pa. Architects Mitchell/Giurgola Associates Architects," *AIA Journal,* May 1974, p. 45.

Goldberger, Paul, "Two cheers for eight winners," *The New York Times,* 2 June 1974, pp. 62-64.

Forman, Nessa, "Local Architect Wins Award," *The Evening Bulletin,* 21 June 1974, pp. 45, 50.

Murray, Robert, "Against the Monument," *Arts Canada,* Autumn 1974, pp. 28-39.

Carlson, Eric, "With a hey and a ho. The Lang Music Building generates an extraordinary amount of music," *Swarthmore College Bulletin,* Alumni Issue, October 1974, pp. 1-3.

"Frightening track meets UDC schedule," *Progressive Architecture,* October 1974, pp. 22-23.

"News Report. Wainwright finalists: 5 out of 47 entries," *Progressive Architecture,* October 1974, p. 29.

Brewster, David, "The Best Modern Architecture in the City," *Argus,* 11 October 1974, p. 1.

Marlin, William, "New U.S. Center: oasis in Brazil's austere capital," *Christian Science Monitor,* 1 November 1974, p. 10.

Hine, Thomas, "In the Center Where History Will Live, Can it Also Sing?" *The Philadelphia Inquirer,* 25 November 1974, Section G, p. 17.

Okada, Shinichi, "Eminent Works Abroad: Contextualism," *Space Design,* December 1974, pp. 47-52.

Stephens, Suzanne, "Between culture and context," *Progressive Architecture,* December 1974, pp. 54-67.

"Going On. Wainwright Winners Announced," *AIA Journal,* December 1974, p. 16.

Longstreth, Richard W. and Edward Teitelman, *Architecture in Philadelphia: A Guide,* MIT Press, Cambridge, MA., 1975.

Moore, Charles W. and Richard B. Oliver, "Architecture," *Encyclopedia Americana Annual,* Americana Corporation, New York, 1975, pp. 97-99.

Hine, Thomas, "Penn Mutual Building: View Changes the Face," *The Philadelphia Inquirer,* 28 February 1975, Section B, p. 2.

Goldberger, Paul, "Elegant Hybrid," *The New York Times Magazine,* 30 March 1975, pp. 58-59, 62.

Franck, Claude, "Le Bon Vieux Temps n'a Pas Disparu: Extension du Siège de la Penn Mutual Insurance Company, Philadelphie," *L'Architecture D'Aujourd'hui,* April 1975, p. XVIII.

Morton, David, "Between town and gown," *Progressive Architecture,* April 1975, pp. 66-71.

"Columbus East High School, Columbus, Ind., Architects: Mitchell/Giurgola Associates," *AIA Journal,* May 1975, pp. 34-35.

"The College Center: A Welcome Addition," *Accent: Plattsburgh State,* Vol. 3, No. 3, Spring/Summer 1975, pp. 6-7.

"Forest Murmurs," *Architectural Review,* June 1975, p. 386.

Rondinella, Dr. Ing. Ruggero, "La sede della United Fund a Filadelfia," *L'Industria Italiana del Cemento,* July/August 1975, pp. 453-462.

Green, Perry, "The Tower Is Rising," *Columbia Engineering PULSE,* 17 September 1975, pp. 1-2.

Forman, Nessa, "View From Top and Inside Story," *Philadelphia Evening Bulletin,* 14 November 1975, pp. 25, 30.

Dallas, Jack, "Redesigned Main Entrance to Open Soon," *The Girard Columns* 26 November 1975, p. 1.

"Mitchell/Giurgola," *Architecture + Urbanism,* December 1975, pp. 61-120.

Goldberger, Paul, "Works of Mitchell/Giurgola," *Architecture + Urbanism,* December 1975, pp. 121-123.

"Symposium, Mitchell/Giurgola, Ten New Designs," *Space Design,* December 1975, pp. 4-84.

Hine, Thomas, "Bell's New Home Meant for Pilgrims," *The Philadelphia Inquirer,* 31 December 1975, Section B, pp. 1-2.

Blake, Peter and Bernard Quint, *Modern Architecture America,* n.p.: United States Information Service, 1976.

Sky, Alison M. Stone, *Unbuilt America: Forgotten Architecture in the United States from Thomas Jefferson to the Space Age,* McGraw Hill, New York, 1976.

Thomas, George, *Philadelphia: Three Centuries of American Art,* The Museum of Art, Philadelphia, 1976, pp. 599-601.

"Work begins on $300-million renewal project," *Engineering News-Record,* 1 January 1976, p. 11.

Eberhard, John P. "Architecture and Energy: The Need for a New Aesthetic," *AIA Journal,* February 1976, pp. 24-27.

Canty, Donald and Dunlop, B., "Post-Renaissance Philadelphia," *AIA Journal,* March 1976, pp. 31-51.

Dean, Andrea O., "Profile of the Firm Award Recipient: Mitchell/Giurgola," *AIA Journal,* April 1976, pp. 58-61.

Marlin, William, "Mitchell/Giurgola Associates: Three Benchmark Buildings," *Architectural Record,* April 1976, pp. 107-118.

Morton, David, "Liberty Bell Pavilion," *Progressive Architecture,* April 1976, p. 65.

————, "Living History Museum," *Progressive Architecture,* April 1976, p. 67.

————, "Of Transitions," *Progressive Architecture,* April 1976, pp. 72-75.

Marlin, William, "Columbus: A City of Rarefied Design," *Christian Science Monitor,* 2 April 1976, p. 27.

Goldberger, Paul, "Prairie Showplace," *The New York Times Magazine,* 4 April 1976, pp. 46-50, 52, 54.

————, "Innovative Firm Puts its Imprint on Philadelphia," *The New York Times,* 6 May 1976, p. 39.

Campbell, Robert, "Giurgola's Philadelphia Trail Blazer," *Boston Sunday Globe,* 30 May 1976, Section E, p. 2.

"Penn Mutual Tower," *Tremco Construction News,* June 1976, pp. 2-3.

"Bell Proclaims Liberty to AIA Throughout the Land. M/G Design Rings True," *F.W. Dodge Construction News,* 4 June 1976, Section I, p. 24.

Russell, Beverly, "America Discovers Columbus," *House & Garden,* July 1976, pp. 80-83, 103.

"Overview of Independence," *Buildings,* July 1976, pp. 36-39.

Steinbruck, Victor, "Seattle Architect Evaluates Concept for Westlake Mall," *Northwest Arts,* 6 August 1976, pp. 1, 6-7.

Douglas, Patrick, "Seattle," *Saturday Review,* 21 August 1976, pp. 10-13.

Davis, Douglas, "Electronic Carnival," *Newsweek,* 30 August 1976, p. 72.

Gebhard, David and Deborah Nevins, *200 years of American Architectural Drawing,* Whitney Library of Design, New York, 1977.

Kaye, Ellen, "Color Scheming," *The Philadelphia Inquirer Today Magazine,* 16 January 1977, pp. 18-20.

"East School Columbus," *Baumeister,* February 1977, p. 136.

Marlin, William, "Structures With A Social Value," *Christian Science Monitor,* 21 April 1977, p. 23.

"The 1977 AIA Honor Awards. Penn Mutual Tower, Philadelphia. Mitchell/Giurgola," *AIA Journal,* May 1977, p. 32.

Hine, Thomas, "Old standards apply in honors for architecture," *The Philadelphia Inquirer,* 22 May 1977, Section L, p. 1.

"College Occupies New $5.9 Million Feinberg Library," *Plattsburgh State Today,* July/August 1977, p. 1.

"Una intervista di Kenneth Frampton a Aldo Giurgola," *Controspazio,* July-August 1977, pp. 54-57.

Hoyt, Charles King, "Relating common solutions: two libraries by Mitchell/Giurgola," *Architectural Record,* August 1977, pp. 93-98.

"St. Joseph's Village, Brookhaven/USA," *Architektur Wettbewerbe,* September 1977, p. 44.

"Mitchell Giurgola Architects," *Process Architecture No. 2,* Special Issue, October 1977.

Goldberger, Paul, "Science Building Marks New Day for Architecture at Columbia U.," *The New York Times,* 25 October 1977, p. 41.

Osborne, Michelle, "Books: The late great King Kahn," Review of *Louis I. Kahn,* by Romaldo Giurgola and Jaimini Mehta, *Philadelphia Magazine,* November 1977, pp. 78-86.

Davern, Jeanne M., "Four U.S. projects under development by Mondev International," *Architectural Record,* December 1977, pp. 96-107.

Hoekema, James, "Drawing Toward Architectural Drawings," *Art Forum,* December 1977, pp. 44-47.

"Ehrman Mitchell, Jr., and Romaldo Giurgola," *Shinkenchiku. A View of Contemporary World Architects,* Shinkenchiku-sha Co. Ltd., Tokyo, December 1977, p. 96.

Huxtable, Ada Louise, "A Stylish New Building at Columbia," *The New York Times,* 11 December 1977, pp. 35-36.

Carpenter, Edward, "Harristown: A New Heart for a Tri-County Community," *Urban Design,* Winter 1977, pp. 15-17.

Heyer, Paul, *Architects on Architecture. New Directions in America,* Walker and Co., New York, 1978.

"Masonry Makes News at Lukens Steel," *Newsletter. Delaware Valley Masonry Institute* 4, No. 1 (1978), p. 1.

"Romaldo Giurgola," *Great Models,* Student publication of School of Design, North Carolina State University, 27 (1978), p. 67-69.

"Citation: Architectural Design. Mitchell/Giurgola Architects," *Progressive Architecture,* January 1978, p. 80.

"Tredyffrin Public Library Wins Award Designed by Mitchell/Giurgola," *Philadelphia Construction News,* 3 January 1978, p. 1.

"Architectural Drawings, Romaldo Giurgola, Retreat in Rural Sweden," *Architectural Digest,* March 1978, p. 81.

Filler, Martin, "Technics: Ceramic Tile. Tile - now and forever," *Progressive Architecture,* March 1978, pp. 94-102.

Filler, Martin, "Hail Columbia," *Progressive Architecture,* March 1978, pp. 54-59.

"News Report. Mitchell/Giurgola office building," *Progressive Architecture,* March 1978, p. 50.

Ramazzotti, Luigi, "USA. Penn Mutual Tower, Philadelphia," *L'Industria delle Construzioni* 77, March 1978, pp. 68-74.

"Library Design Endorsed," *The University Gazette. The University of North Carolina at Chapel Hill* 6, No. 9, 5 May 1978, pp. 1-2.

Miller, Nory, "Welcoming Place to Read and Reflect," *AIA Journal,* Mid-May 1978, pp. 90-95.

Goldberger, Paul, "Diversity Marks Architecture Awards," *The New York Times,* 6 June 1978, Section B, pp. 1, 17.

"Graduate Studies Center Site to be Dedicated," *The American College Today,* 7, No. 2 (July 1978), pp. 1, 4.

Kaye, Ellen, "Conquering Vast Spaces," *The Philadelphia Inquirer Today Magazine,* 3 September 1978, pp. 18-19.

"Auditorium Architect Selected," *University Bulletin, LIU* VII, No. 1 (Fall 1978), p. 1.

Morton, David, "State University College Library, Plattsburgh, NY. Unmessy Vitality," *Progressive Architecture,* October 1978, pp. 80-83.

Downey, Roger, "A Museum Grows on Westlake," *The Weekly, Seattle's News Magazine,* 4-10 October 1978, pp. 25-26.

"Tile Faced Precast Panels Speed Construction, While Giving A Hand-Laid Look," *Architectural Record,* Mid-October 1978, pp. 14-16.

"Architecture for Adjustment. Building Today in Historical Surroundings," *Baumeister,* December 1978, p. 1115.

"Sherman Fairchild Center for the Life Sciences," *Space Design,* December 1978, pp. 102.

"A design architect takes helm at AIA," *Engineering News-Record,* 7 December 1978, pp. 32-34.

Clark, Roger H. and Michael Pause and twenty students of the School of Design, "Analysis of Precedent," *The Student Publication of the School of Design North Carolina State University at Raleigh* 28, 1979.

"Graduate Studies Center Complex Scheduled for Occupancy in '81," *The American College Today,* April 1979, pp. 1, 2, 3.

"Tredyffrin's Arc," *American Libraries,* May 1979, p. 253.

"A Celebration of Architecture. Interview with AIA President Ehrman B. Mitchell, Jr.," *Constructor,* June 1979, pp. 24-25, 54, 56.

Bell, David, "Unity and Aesthetics of Incompletion in Architecture," *Architectural Design,* July 1979, pp. 175-182.

Schulze, Franz, "On Campus Architecture," *Portfolio,* August/September 1979, pp. 34-39.

Kaye, Ellen, "A Gallery for Living," *The Philadelphia Inquirer Today Magazine,* 7 October, 1979, pp. 26-27.

Andrews, Ross, "Prizewinners chosen for Parliament House design," *The Canberra Times,* 10 October 1979, p. 1.

"Giurgola, Romaldo," *Contemporary Architects,* St. Martin's Press, New York, 1980, pp. 285-287, 551.

"Mitchell, Ehrman B.," *Contemporary Architects,* St. Martin's Press, New York, 1980, p. 551.

"City Segments," *Design Quarterly* 113-114, 1980, pp. 36-37.

"New York: State University of New York, College at Plattsburgh," *Library Journal,* Special Report No. 16 (1980), pp. 40-44.

Pennsylvania Avenue Development Corporation/1980 Annual Report, Pennsylvania Avenue Development Corporation, Washington, D.C., 1980.

"News Report. Lafayette Place, Boston, Ma.," *Progressive Architecture,* January 1980, p. 38.

Jenning, Steve, "Designers present 3 building plans to jury of citizens," *The Oregonian,* 16 February 1980, Section A, p. 17.

"A Stimulating Environment for Professional Growth," *The American College Today,* April 1980, pp. 7-8.

"News Report. Portland competition a very public issue," *Progressive Architecture,* May 1980, p. 25.

Sides, Carol, "Winning House 'Buried' in Capital Hill," *The Canberra Times,* 27 June 1980, p. 1.

Wanner, Dick, "A House that Works," *Sunday News* (Lancaster, Pa.), 6 July 1980, Section 5, p. 1.

Hine, Thomas, "A Winning Design for Australia," *The Philadelphia Inquirer,* 20 July 1980, Section I, pp. 1, 2.

Dean, Andrea O., "How Competitors View Competitions," *AIA Journal,* August 1980, pp. 56-60.

"Parliament House," *Architecture Australia,* September 1980, pp. 36-50.

"The winning design and the Griffin Plan," *Architecture Australia,* September 1980, pp. 51-52.

"Concert Theater Grows on Campus," *Posthaste, LIU* 9, No. 1 (Fall 1980), p. 1.

"Australian Parliament," *Oculus on current New York architecture* 42, No. 1, October 1980, pp. 1, 4-5.

Old and New Architecture: Design Relationship, National Trust for Historic Preservation, Washington, D.C., October 1980.

Korzeniewski, Swetik and Douglas Little, "The Parliament House Design," *Transition* 1, No. 4, November 1980, pp. 42-43.

Hine, Thomas, "Philadelphia: An Architecture Tour," *Portfolio,* December 1980, pp. 108-111.

"Post-Modern Parliament," *Architectural Review,* December 1980, pp. 354-359.

Yee, Roger, "A New Urban Center for Harrisburg," *Architectural Record,* December 1980, pp. 76-81.

Davern, Jeanne and editors, *Architecture: 1970-1980 A Decade of Change,* Architectural Record, New York, 1981.

Goldstein, Barbara and Esther McCoy, *Guide to U.S. Architecture 1940-1980,* Arts and Architecture Press, Santa Monica, CA., 1981.

"Le nouveau complexe parlementaire de Canberra," *Recherche & Architecture,* 1981, p. 45.

Robertson, Jaquelin T., "Canberra," *Oculus,* January 1981, p. 7.

Davis, Douglas, "An Invisible Parliament," *Newsweek,* 26 January 1981, pp. 73-74.

Marlin, William, "Australia's new Parliament House," *Inland Architect,* January/February 1981, pp. 23-39.

Taylor, Jennifer with Edmund Bacon and Jacquelin Robertson, "Canberra," *Progressive Architecture,* March 1981, pp. 23-39.

Arieff, Irwin B., "Capital Hill: Everybody Has Designs on its Future," *Congressional Quarterly,* 28 March 1981, pp. 539-541.

"Downtown Development Awards. Harristown Phase I," *Architectural Record,* April 1981, p. 45.

"Building Documentation: International House, Westlake Park," *The Harvard Architecture Review* 2, Spring 1981, pp. 163-171.

A.I.D. Regional Office Friuli, *The U.S. Assistance Program in Italy's Friuli Region Following the Earthquakes of 1976,* A.I.D. Regional Office Friuli, New York, 6 May 1981.

"Parliament House 1988," *Canberra '81,* June 1981, pp. 18-22.

Goldberger, Paul, "An 1891 'Skyscraper' Reigns Over a Block of St. Louis," *The New York Times,* 6 July 1981, p. 8.

"C. W. Post: Versatility in Concrete," *Concrete Industry Bulletin,* Summer 1981, p. 4.

Day, Norman, "Australian Perspective on Mitchell Giurgola's Parliament House," *Express,* Summer 1981, p. 20.

Knight III, Carleton, "Wainwright rededicated a state office complex," *Preservation News,* August 1981, pp. 1, 18.

Goodman, Peter, "Sounding Optimistic at C. W. Post," *Newsday,* 2 August 1981, Part II, p. 33.

Kazanski, Boris, "Das Neue Parlamentsgebaude in Canberra, Australien," *Architektur + Wettbewerbe,* September 1981, pp. 29-32.

Seligsohn, Leo, "Long Island's Great New Hall of Plenty," *LI/Newsday's Magazine for Long Island,* 27 September 1981, pp. 10-14, 41, 43.

"Mitchell/Giurgola Kasperson Residence," *GA Houses: New Waves in American Architecture 2,* October 1981, pp. 50-53.

Delatiner, Barbara, "Post's New Concert Hall Is Test for Arts," *The New York Times/Long Island Weekly,* 4 October 1981, Section II, pp. 1, 11.

Kaufman, Bill, "The Hall Rang to the Sound of Bravo," *Newsday,* 12 October 1981, Part II, pp. 4, 5.

McCue George, "Spirit from St. Louis," *Progressive Architecture,* November 1981, pp. 102-106.

Brenner, Douglas, "Mitchell/Giurgola Build A Gateway to Stamford," *Architectural Record,* December 1981, pp. 86-91.

Dillon, David, "AIA Medal didn't tarnish over time," *The Dallas Morning News,* 10 December 1981, Section C, p. 17.

Campbell, Robert, "Boston. Wealth of new hotels shapes up with the emphasis on wealth," *The Boston Globe,* 27 December 1981, Section A, pp. 1, 2.

Filler, Martin, "Mitchell/Giurgola: C.W. Post Concert Theater," *Skyline,* January 1982, p. 22.

"Giurgola Selected as AIA's 43rd Gold Medalist," *AIA Journal,* January 1982, pp. 13, 16.

Goldberger, Paul, "AIA Medal Gives a Clue to Architecture's Other Agendas," *The New York Times,* The Week in Review, 3 January 1982, Section IV, p. 8.

"Mitchell/Giurgola," *Macmillan Encyclopedia of Architects,* Vol. 3, Macmillan Publishing Co., Inc., New York, 1982, pp. 209-210.

Von Eckardt, Wolf, "Creating Good-Looking Objects that Work," *Time,* 4 January 1982, pp. 74-75.

Ryder, Sharon Lee, "Tonic to Dominant," *Metropolis,* January/February 1982, p. 5.

Filler, Martin, "Why Modesty is the Best Policy," *House & Garden,* March 1982, p. 10.

Miller, Joanne, "Whitaker College, Health Services Complex to be dedicated on Friday," *Tech Talk,* 3 March 1982, pp. 1, 8.

Zevi, Bruno, "Non contestate il contesto," *L'Espresso,* 28 March 1982, p. 143.

Pearson, Clifford, "Of Country Estates and Corporate Architecture," *Metropolis,* May 1982, pp. 9-11.

Lowry, Shannon, "Designers work on museum plan," *Anchorage Times,* 2 May 1982, p. 1.

"Giurgola Wins AIA Gold Medal," *F. W. Dodge Construction News,* 7 May 1982, pp. 3-4.

Abercrombie, Stanley, "The Wainwright: Building on Genius," *AIA Journal,* Mid-May 1982, pp. 162-169.

Forgey, Benjamin, "Pennsylvania Avenue," *The Washington Post,* 23 May 1982, Section K, pp. 1, 4, 5.

"Anchorage Historical and Fine Arts Museum, Mitchell/Giurgola Architects," *Skyline,* June 1982, p. 19.

Forsht, James L., "In Harmony. Unifying Interior and Exterior," *Architectural Digest,* June 1982, pp. 144-149.

Stephens, Suzanne, "Notes of an Armchair Museumgoer," *Skyline,* June 1982, p. 18.

Dillon, David, "Giurgola's work shows his concern for people's needs," *The Dallas Morning News,* 20 June 1982, Section C, pp. 1, 9.

"Giurgola: Architecture Should Be An Extension of the Environment," *AIA Journal,* July 1982, p. 16.

"Giurgola receives Gold Medal," *F.W. Dodge Construction News,* 16 July 1982, pp. 41-42.

Knobel, Lance, "Giurgola in Friuli," *The Architectural Review,* August 1982, pp. 28-35.

"Architecture is hard work, Gold Medalist Giurgola reminds convention," *Architectural Record,* August 1982, p. 71.

Murphy, Jim, "Out of Round," *Progressive Architecture,* August 1982, pp. 49-53.

"Wainwright-Gebaude in St. Louis," *Baumeister,* September 1982, pp. 860-864.

Fox, Arthur, "Parliament House hits stride," *Engineering News-Record,* 25 November 1982, pp. 22-24.

BIBLIOGRAPHY OF WRITINGS BY R. GIURGOLA

Giurgola, Romaldo, "Eric Mendelsohn 1887-1953," *Interiors,* December 1953, pp. 76-77.

————, "Architecture in Change," *Journal of Architectural Education,* vol. 17, November-December 1962, pp. 104-106.

————, "Early Stages in an Idea in Architecture," *Dimension* 15, Spring 1964, pp. 16-25.

————, "Reflections on Buildings and the City: The Realism of the Partial Vision," *Perspecta* 9/10, 1965, pp. 107-130.

————, "Romaldo Giurgola on Louis Kahn," *Zodiac* 17, 1967, p. 119.

————, "A Propos de Louis Kahn," *L'Architecture D'Aujourd'hui,* February-March 1969, pp. 4-5.

————, "The Discreet Charm of the Bourgeoisie," *Architectural Forum,* May 1973, pp. 56-57.

————, "Louis I. Kahn, 1901-1974," *Progressive Architecture,* May 1974, pp. 4-5.

————, "Architecture is both image and reality . . . ," *Space Design,* December 1975, pp. 2-3.

————, and J. Mehta, *Louis I. Kahn,* Westview Press, Boulder, Colo., 1975.

————, "Design and Planning: Alvar Aalto," *Progressive Architecture,* April 1977, pp. 53-57.

————, "The Impetus to Build," *Christian Science Monitor,* 21 April 1977, pp. 24-25.

————. "Nuovi indirizzi progettuali in U.S.A.," *Laboratorio* 2, September-November 1977, pp. 35-37.

————, "The Aesthetic of Place," *Process Architecture* No. 2, October 1977, pp. 34-37.

————, *Roma Interrotta,* Incontri Internationali d'Arte, Rome, 1979, pp. 118-128.

————, "Drawings: The Villa Imperiale," *Precis,* Vol I (1979), pp. 26-27.

————, "Answers to some questions that we didn't quite ask," *AIA Journal,* Mid-May 1979, pp. 161-162.

————, "L'edilizia industriale negli Stati Uniti," *Laboratorio* 6-7, July-December 1979, pp. 7-13.

————, "Utzon, Jørn," *Contemporary Architects,* St. Martin's Press, New York, 1980, pp. 829-831.

————, "Valle, Gino," *Contemporary Architects,* St. Martin's Press, New York, 1980, pp. 835-836.

————, "Venturi, Robert," *Contemporary Architects,* St. Martin's Press, New York, 1980, pp. 848-850.

————, "Notes on Architecture and Morality," *Precis,* Vol. II (1980), pp. 51-52.

————, "Design Precepts and the Building Form," *Parliament House, Canberra,* Fall 1980.

————, "The Producing Moment," *Inland Architect,* January/February 1981, pp. 39-42.

————, "Notes on Buildings and Their Parts," *The Harvard Architectural Review,* Spring 1981, pp. 172-175.

————, "Giurgola on Kahn," *AIA Journal,* August 1982, pp. 27-35.

————, with Pamille I. Berg, "Kahn, Louis I.," *Macmillan Encyclopedia of Architects* Vol. 2, Macmillan Publishing Co. Inc., New York, pp. 537-546.

INDEX